Dublin Street Names

Dublin Street Names

Paul Clerkin

Gill & Macmillan

Gill & Macmillan Ltd
Hume Avenue
Park West
Dublin 12

with associated companies throughout the world
www.gillmacmillan.ie

© 2001 Paul Clerkin
0 7171 3204 8

Print origination by Andy Gilsenan, Dublin
Printed by The Guernsey Press, Guernsey

A catalogue record is available for this book from the British Library.

5 4 3 2 1

Contents

ABBEY STREET

Divided into Upper, Middle and Lower Abbey Streets, this is one of the main thoroughfares of the city and was already an important street in 1756 when Rocque's map described it as Great Abbey Street and Little Abbey Street. The street derives its name from the medieval St Mary's Abbey, founded in 1139, which was affiliated to the monastery of Savigny in Normandy before coming under the Cistercian order in 1147. The lands of St Mary's were substantial, stretching as far as the Tolka River, and the wealth of the abbey meant that its buildings were amongst the finest in Dublin, used for meetings of the English Council of State and other bodies. It was in the chapter house, at a meeting of the Privy Council, that 'Silken' Thomas Fitzgerald renounced his allegiance to Henry VIII and began the unsuccessful rebellion of 1534. After the abbey was closed in 1539 with the suppression of the monasteries, the buildings were dismantled and the stones used for other purposes in the city, including the construction of the original Essex Bridge. During the late 19th century the chapter house was rediscovered intact under buildings off Little Mary Street. It is the only part of the abbey visible today, and is open to the public.

MIDDLE ABBEY STREET has long been associated with newspaper publishing. The nationalist newspaper, *The Nation*, was published here, on the site marked by a plaque on the wall of the offices of Independent Newspapers.

LOWER ABBEY STREET is the location of the famous Abbey Theatre, founded in 1904 as the Irish National Theatre Company, and originally housed in a building purchased from the Mechanics Institute. On the night of 18 July 1951, the Abbey was badly damaged by fire. The replacement building designed by Michael Scott and Partners (Scott was himself a former Abbey actor) was opened on a larger site on Abbey Street in 1966. It is now proposed that this building be replaced or substantially renovated. The façade of the original building was salvaged by architect Dáithí Hanley.

ABERCORN ROAD / SQUARE / TERRACE
Part of the North Lotts scheme, Abercorn Road was laid out in the 1860s and takes its name from James Hamilton, Duke of Abercorn, who was Lord Lieutenant during the periods 1866–8 and 1874–6.

ABERDEEN STREET
Named after the Earl of Aberdeen, Lord Lieutenant, who opened the schemes of houses built here by the Dublin Artisans' Dwellings Company. Founded in 1876, the Artisans' Dwellings Company was responsible for many such schemes in the city including those at Harold's Cross, Manor Street, Portobello, Plunkett Street, Seville Place and Pimlico. It was run on business principles rather than as a charity, and by 1907 had 2,961 dwellings, each with water supply and water closet, generating a yearly rent of £40,000.

ADELAIDE ROAD
Named after Queen Adelaide (1792–1849), wife of William IV. Before being renamed in 1833 this was known as Old Circular Road and was so marked on maps. The road is best known to generations for the Royal Victoria Eye and Ear Hospital, an imposing brick building occupying most of the north side.

Designed by Carroll and Bachelor, it was completed in 1901 after twenty-six years of construction. The façade has recently been cleaned. The fine Presbyterian Church that completes the vista from the east side of St Stephen's Green up Earlsfort Terrace was designed by an unknown architect around 1840, with a later façade by H. J. Lundy. The Ionic portico, stern and forbidding, leads directly into the organ gallery. The building is now under threat of demolition from the Presbyterian Synod.

ALDBOROUGH PLACE / SQUARE / PARADE

These are all in the neighbourhood of Aldborough House, home of Edward Stratford, Viscount Amiens, who was created first Earl of Aldborough in 1777. The house was constructed in 1796 at a cost of £40,000, with a central block and two small wings. It was the last of the great houses to be built in the city centre. By the early 19th century the building was being used as a school known as the Feinaglian Institute, run by a Professor von Feinagle who renamed the house Luxembourg. A telecommunications company now uses it.

ALEXANDRA BASIN / QUAY / ROAD

Named after Alexandra, Princess of Wales, wife of the future Edward VII, who formally opened the basin in 1885. Alexandra Quay was finished in 1931. Nearby Alexandra Road is the main route through this area of the Dublin docks.

ALFIE BYRNE ROAD

Alfie Byrne (1882–1956) was an important figure in Dublin public life for forty-four years. He was first elected to Dublin City Council in 1912; this was followed by election to the Westminster Parliament in 1914. After Independence, he was elected to Dáil Éireann from 1922 to 1928, and again from 1932 to 1956. He was a member of the Seanad from 1928 to 1932. Alfie Byrne's most impressive civic achievement, however, lay in holding the office of Lord Mayor of Dublin continuously between 1930 and 1939, and for a final term in 1954–5. His tireless campaigning for more playgrounds for Dublin, combined with his legendary children's parties in the Mansion House, won him the unofficial title of 'the children's Lord Mayor'. When he died in 1956 the adulatory obituaries in the newspapers of the day reflected the general affection in which citizens held him. Alfie Byrne Road is built across reclaimed land to link the North Lotts with Clontarf.

AMIENS STREET

So named around 1800 after Viscount Amiens, first Earl of Aldborough, whose family home was nearby. It was originally known as the Strand, because of its coastal route. Previous to this the name Amiens Street had been applied to the eastern end of what is now Seán Mac Dermott Street. The street also gave its name to one of Dublin's four main railway termini. Amiens Street Station was constructed for the Drogheda and Dublin Railway Company between 1844 and 1846, and was the first of the four termini to be completed. It was built on an axis with Talbot Street, which allows the central tower, visible the length of that street, to act as a signpost to travellers. Its symmetrical five-bay façade has three towers and an enormous entrance arch. The station is still in use today, and although renamed Connolly Station in 1966 after James Connolly, who was executed for his part in the 1916 rising, it is still sometimes referred to by its old name. It has recently been extended and renovated by Córas Iompair Éireann Architects.

ANDREW'S LANE

Derives its name from St Andrew's Church, which was the chapel for the Irish Parliament based in College Green. The current building (now a tourist centre) was built in the 1860s after a fire destroyed the 'Round Church' built between 1670 and 1674.

ANGLESEA STREET

This was developed on the estate of Lord Arthur Annesley, created first Earl of Anglesea in 1661, who leased the lands that lay between his house on Dame Street and the Liffey from Dublin Corporation in 1657–62. The street is best known as the location of the Irish Stock Exchange. The Exchange is contained behind a very sedate and unremarkable exterior, concealing an intact Italianate galleried interior. Two good examples of the Queen Anne Revival style can be seen in Nos. 10 and 28, which were built in 1898 and 1895 and have very elaborate shop fronts. The architect(s) of these two buildings is unknown.

ANNE STREET NORTH

Originally the land here belonged to St Anne's Guild, the guild of bakers. It is mentioned in 1581 as 'S. Anne's ground without Newgate', and is part of the Smithfield markets area. Anne Street North contains some of the great stone former warehouses of the nearby Jameson Distillery, which have now been converted to apartments. Until recently a run-down area, the street has become rejuvenated in recent years.

ANNE STREET SOUTH

A busy commercial street linking Grafton Street and Dawson Street, it was laid out by Joshua Dawson and takes its name from St Anne's Church in Dawson Street.

ANNESLEY BRIDGE

Named after Richard Annesley, a director of the Royal Canal Company in 1791.

ARBOUR HILL / ARBOUR HILL PLACE / ARBOUR HILL TERRACE

The name is derived from the Irish *Cnoc an Arbhair* (corn hill) as the area was partially owned by Christ Church Cathedral in medieval times and was used for the storage of corn. The Stoneybatter end of Arbour Hill betrays its country-lane origins with a winding course and small cottages, while the other end is dominated by the rear of Collins Barracks and by Arbour Hill Prison. The smallest of Dublin's Victorian prisons, Arbour Hill was designed in 1835 by Jacob Owen, and was later rebuilt in 1845 by Sir Joshua Webb. It has a tripartite façade; the central entrance block is linked by screen walls to the chapel and to the governor's house. Of these buildings the most interesting is the chapel, with its elaborate cruciform interior and roof, and behind the altar, stained glass from the Harry Clarke Studios. It has an unusual entrance porch with stairs leading to twin galleries for visitors in the nave and transept. This feature was copied from the National Scotch Church in Bow Street in London, designed by Robert Wallace. Another unusual feature is the Celtic round tower rising from a rectangular base.

Legend has it that Little John (of Robin Hood fame) came to Dublin in medieval times and amazed the local people with his ability with a bow and arrow. According to Walker's *Historical Memories of the Irish Bards*:

> 'According to tradition, Little John (who followed his master to this country) shot an arrow from the old bridge (now Church Street bridge) to the present site of St Michan's Church, a distance of about 11 score and seven yards, but poor Little John's great practical skill in archery could not save him from an ignominious fate; as it appears from the records of the Southwell family, he was publicly executed for robbery on Arbour Hill.'

ARD RIGH ROAD

Part of a naming pattern of streets of small houses developed by the Artisans' Dwellings Company in this area near Arbour Hill. The pattern is based on Norse and Irish history and mythology, and the name Ard Righ refers to the High Kings of Ireland.

ARDEE STREET / ROW

Previously known as Crooked Staff, Ardee Street was renamed after Sir Edward Brabazon, Baron Ardee, whose son William was created Earl of Meath in 1627. Some of the surrounding streets – Earl Street North, Meath Street and Brabazon Street – are also named after the family. This collective naming of streets, reflecting the influence of certain families, is a common pattern in Dublin. The Brabazon family owned a lot of property in this part of the city as an ancestor, William Brabazon, was granted the Abbey of St Thomas the Martyr in 1545, and the area became the Earl of Meath's Liberties. The name 'the Liberties' is still used to describe this area.

ARDILAUN TERRACE

Just off the North Circular Road and named after Sir Arthur Guinness, Lord Ardilaun. Ardilaun is an island in Lough Corrib beside the former Guinness residence of Ashford Castle.

ARNOTT STREET

Laid out as a residential street off the South Circular Road in 1873. It was named after Sir John Arnott, the industrialist and owner of *The Irish Times*, who developed the area together with James Lombard and Edward McMahon, after whom streets are also named.

ARRAN QUAY / ARRAN STREET EAST

Named after Charles Butler, Earl of Arran and brother of James, Duke of Ormonde, who was Lord Lieutenant for three periods: 1644–9, 1662–9 and 1677–85. Part of Arran Street East was previously known as Boot Lane after an inn of that name.

Largely rebuilt with apartments in the 1990s, Arran Quay contains the fine St Paul's Church, which dates from 1835–7and was designed by Patrick Byrne. It has an impressive portico with four Ionic columns fronting the river. The tower was completed in 1843; it enables the church to be seen the length of the quays except from the east, where the view is blocked by the dome of the Four Courts.

The statesman and political philosopher Edmund Burke (1729–97) was born at No. 12, now demolished. Burke was the son of a mixed marriage but was brought up in the Church of Ireland. Educated at Trinity College, he studied law in the Middle Temple in London but failed to be called to the bar. Between 1765 and 1780 he was an MP at Westminster, while also writing articles for the *Annual Register*. A great orator, he opened the impeachment trial of Warren Hastings, the first Governor-General of India, with a speech that lasted four days. A bronze statue of Burke stands outside Trinity College near that of his friend Oliver Goldsmith.

ASDILL'S ROW
Leading from Crampton Quay to Temple Bar, this first appeared as an unnamed lane on Brooking's map of 1728. Rocque showed it as a narrow gated laneway in 1756.

ASTON QUAY / PLACE
Major Henry Aston was given permission to develop this frontage along the Liffey in 1680. By 1708 the quay was known as Aston's Quay. Aston Place was called Lee's Lane on Rocque's map of 1756 and in the OS of 1838.

AUBURN STREET
Named after the hamlet commemorated in Oliver Goldsmith's famous poem, 'The Deserted Village'. Nearby Goldsmith Street bears his name.

AUGHRIM STREET / PLACE / VILLAS / LANE

So named to mark the centenary of the Battle of Aughrim, which took place in 1691 in Co. Galway. Aughrim Street was originally part of Blackhorse Lane.

AUNGIER STREET

Once the site of several churches, Aungier Street was named after Sir Francis Aungier, Master of the Rolls, who acquired the lands of the White Friar Monastery situated here. The street was driven through an oval plot of land which had never been built on because it was marshy, and on old maps and plans, before it was built, the surrounding streets can be seen to curve around the area. Sir Francis Aungier's daughter Alice married Sir James Cuffe, whose name was given to nearby Cuffe Street.

The poet Thomas Moore (1779–1852) was born at No. 12 Aungier Street. Moore was educated at the famous Whyte's Academy at 79 Grafton Street, now more famous as the site of Bewley's Cafe. Amongst other students at the school were Richard Brinsley Sheridan; Arthur Wellesley, Duke of Wellington; and Robert Emmet, with whom Moore remained friends until Emmet's execution. Moore was later educated at Trinity College after partial repeal of the Penal Laws allowed him as a Catholic to do so. He spent most of the rest of his life away from Dublin, visiting it frequently. He was a friend of Lord Byron's and was responsible for destroying Byron's memoirs after his death at the behest of Byron's relatives.

The Victorian writer Joseph Sheridan Le Fanu wrote a short story of ghostly happenings entitled 'An Account of Some Disturbances in Aungier Street'.

AVONDALE ROAD

Named after Avondale, Co. Wicklow, the residence of Charles Stewart Parnell.

BACHELOR'S WALK

So named not – as is widely suggested – because it was used as a promenade by bachelors, but after a property developer who built here when the quays were extended downstream from Ormond Quay in the 1670s. There have been many variations on the name over the years – Batchelours Walke (1728), The Batchelors Walk (1723 and 1728), and Bachelors Quay (1766). Before the extension of what is now O'Connell Street to the river, Bachelor's Walk extended over part of Eden Quay, ending at what was Union Lane, now part of Marlborough Street. In 1914, a detachment of the King's Own Scottish Borderers fired on a crowd here while returning to barracks. Four people were killed and many others injured. The artist Jack B. Yeats later marked the event with the painting 'Bachelor's Walk, In Memoriam'.

BACK LANE

Runs behind High Street, the main thoroughfare of the medieval city. Another street with the very similar name of Behind Street was once located nearby, behind Skinners Row (now Christchurch Place) but is now extinct. At one time, Back Lane was named Rochell Street or Rochel Lane, a name recently resurrected and given to a nearby apartment block. In the early 1600s, the Jesuits ran a small Catholic university and chapel here, the assets of which were transferred to Trinity College in 1630. Back Lane is the location of the last remaining guild hall in Dublin – Tailor's Hall, now the home of An Taisce, the Irish National Trust. Recent widening of High Street has removed the buildings to the rear of Tailor's Hall and it has now become much more visible. Prior to this, concealed behind a high wall and ornate gateway, it was a little known element of old Dublin. The building, two storeys over basement, has a hall lit on both sides by high round-topped windows, with smaller rooms on two floors. It was used in 1792 for the so-called 'Back Lane Parliament', the meeting of the Catholic Committee organised by Theobald Wolfe Tone.

BAGGOT STREET / COURT / LANE

Named after Robert, Lord Bagod, who was given the Manor of Rath in the 13th century. Baggot Rath Castle stood at what is now the junction of Waterloo Road and Baggot Street. A skirmish was fought here in 1649 between the Lord Lieutenant, the Duke of Ormonde and Cromwell's parliamentary forces. Until around 1756, this was known simply as 'The Road to Ball's Bridge', and as late as 1800 Upper Baggot Street was still known as 'The Blackrock Road'.

Baggot Street is divided into two sections, each with a different architectural character. Baggot Street Lower is mainly Georgian, with some more recent interventions, while Baggot Street Upper is Victorian in style, with many Victorian façades and shopfronts along the northern side, including a fine chemist's. The southern side of the street has been much altered.

The Bank of Ireland in Baggot Street Lower, its visible architecture aside, is most notable for two things: the quantity of bronze manganese used in building it – so much that it affected the price on the world market – and the passions aroused by its construction. The bank went to great lengths to carry out the project in the face of huge opposition, and the building, adored by architects, is almost universally loathed by the public and is at complete odds with Georgian Baggot Street. It consists of three blocks, the first started in 1968 and the last completed in 1978, sited around a courtyard complete with bright steel sculpture. The two smaller four-storey side blocks funnel the viewer towards the main block of eight storeys, approached via a flight of steps. The use of brown-coloured cladding and tinted glass helps minimise the building's impact but the basic impression is of a huge leviathan shoehorned into the street. Designed by Ronald Tallon of Scott Tallon Walker, a great advocate of the style of Mies van der Rohe, the building is an unashamed homage to Mies with its external steelwork and expressionless minimalist façade.

The artist Francis Bacon was born at No. 63 Lower Baggot Street. His former studio has recently been acquired by the Hugh Lane Gallery in Parnell Square. Also in this street are some of Dublin's more famous pubs. The mix of politicians, journalists and economists who frequented Doheny and Nesbitt's in the 1980s led to the coining of the phrase 'the Doheny and Nesbitt School of Economics'. Toner's is a traditional Irish pub, alleged to be the only one ever visited by W. B. Yeats. According to the story, Yeats was brought here by Oliver St John Gogarty. After finishing a sherry he rose to his feet and said, 'I have seen a pub – now, will you kindly take me home.'

BALFE STREET
Named after Michael Balfe (1808–70), violinist and composer, who was born at No. 10 and who wrote 'The Bohemian Girl' and 'The Sicilian Bride', amongst other operas. The street was originally part of Harry Street according to Rocque's map of 1756, but was renamed Pitt Street after William Pitt, son of the first Earl of Chatham.

BALLYBOUGH ROAD
Derived from the Irish *Baile Bocht* 'Town of the poor'.

BARROW STREET

Near the Grand Canal Docks, it takes its name from the river Barrow, which is connected to the Grand Canal navigation system.

BASIN STREET

Named in 1756 after the City Basin, which is located off nearby James's Street. The basin was constructed in 1728 to supply the expanding city with water.

BATH LANE

Named after the baths opened here in 1820 by Sir Arthur Clarke, known for their medicinal value. The baths later operated under Sir James Murray, who patented Fluid Magnesia.

BEAVER STREET / ROW

Of unknown origin, Beaver Street was part of the notorious 'Monto' district of Dublin in the 19th century. Beaver Row in Donnybrook is believed to have derived from a hat factory that was sited there, but there is no evidence to suggest something similar for Beaver Street.

BEDFORD ROW

Of unknown origin but probably named after a local property-owner, or after the Lord Lieutenant of 1756, the Duke of Bedford, whose name was given to the Bedford Tower in Dublin Castle. Bedford Row is shown as Porter's Row in Rocque's map of 1756.

BELVEDERE ROAD / COURT / PLACE / AVENUE

Belvedere Place is named after George Rochfort (1738–1814), second Earl of Belvedere, whose residence Belvedere House stood on nearby Great Denmark Street.

BENBURB STREET

Named for the Battle of Benburb in Co. Armagh in 1646, in

which the Gaelic Irish led by Owen Roe O'Neill defeated the armies led by the Scottish commander Robert Munro, who lost 2,000–3,000 men. Originally named Barrack Street because of its proximity to the former Royal (now Collins) Barracks, it was renamed in 1890 when Barrack Street and Tighe Street were amalgamated. Tighe Street was the eastern end of Benburb Street near Queen Street. It was known as the Gravel Walk until around 1780, and was then renamed after Richard Tighe, who owned property here.

Collins Barracks is the oldest inhabited barracks in Europe and was once one of the largest. It was erected in 1701 on a site that had been earmarked by a hopeful City Corporation for a mansion for the Duke of Ormonde. The Corporation had wanted Ormonde to build here to encourage development on this part of the city. With the exception of the Royal Hospital Kilmainham, this is the earliest classical public building existing in Dublin. The barracks was built to the designs of Thomas Burgh (1670–1730), becoming his first recorded building. Burgh was also responsible for the Custom House (1707), which was replaced by Gandon's masterpiece in 1791; Steevens' Hospital; the Library at Trinity College; and St Werburgh's Church (1715).

BERESFORD PLACE / STREET

The Right Honourable John Beresford was the chief Wide Streets Commissioner and responsible for bringing James Gandon to Ireland. In his role as First Commissioner of Revenue, Beresford had apartments in the northern part of the Custom House, from which he would have been able to see the terrace of houses that today bears his name.

Before the construction of the Custom House, the area from Eden Quay to the North Strand followed the irregular shoreline of the river estuary. Because it was felt by the Wide Streets Commissioners that this should be rectified, Abbey Street Lower and Eden Quay were driven straight through from Sackville Street to end in Beresford Terrace, whose crescent extended to the river by 1838. It was not until the 1950s, however, that this crescent around the rear of the Custom House was completed, when the construction of Memorial Road joined the eastern end of Beresford Place to the quays at the site of the future Matt Talbot Bridge.

There was also discussion about constructing a new avenue to radiate from the Custom House to the Royal Barracks (now Collins Barracks) nearly two miles away. The other street intersecting with the crescent – Store Street West – was placed on an axis originating in the dome of the Custom House. At the time of the construction of the Custom House, this area was largely unbuilt land, and Store Street was laid out merely for symmetry as a short street equal in width to Gardiner Street, in much the same way that Mountjoy Place was created as a cul-de-sac off Mountjoy Square by the Gardiner family.

BERESFORD TERRACE is a short curving terrace of five houses, also built on an axis with the dome of the Custom House. The terrace was designed by James Gandon in 1790, and although in execution much simplified from his designs, it still shows his vision for the setting of the Custom House. The houses are much delapidated externally, and the interiors are relatively unremarkable. This terrace is now the only surviving example in Dublin of a unified housing scheme dating from the 1790s, although many such schemes were approved by the Wide Streets Commissioners. A project by Michael Scott and Partners to demolish the block and replace it with a bronze office block in the 1960s never materialised.

BERESFORD STREET was known as Phrapper or Frapper Lane from the times of Queen Elizabeth I until 1774.

BERKELEY STREET

Formerly known as Somerset Place and later named after Bishop George Berkeley (1685–1753), who was born in Co. Kilkenny and educated at Trinity College, where he was admitted as a Fellow in 1707 and acted as Librarian for a time. The new Berkeley Library was named after him in the 1970s. After a spell in England, Berkeley returned to Ireland as Dean of Dromore and later became Dean of Derry. He went to America in 1728 to attempt to found a missionary college in Bermuda. When this failed he returned to Ireland and eventually became Bishop of Cloyne.

BESSBOROUGH AVENUE

Named after the Lord Lieutenant of 1846–7, the fourth Earl of Bessborough. Bessborough is a small village in Co. Armagh.

BETHESDA LANE

Named after the Bethseda Chapel, which was converted to a cinema in 1913 and is now the site of the Waxworks Museum.

BINNS' BRIDGE

Crossing the Royal Canal at Drumcondra, it is named after John Binns, a director of the Royal Canal Company in 1791.

BISHOP STREET

Named because of its proximity to the Palace of Saint Sepulchre, the residence until 1815 of the Archbishop of Dublin. Many of the streets in the vicinity reflect the religious associations of the area around St Patrick's Cathedral. In Rocque's map of 1756, this was Great Boater Lane (also referred to as Big Boater Lane), possibly from the Irish *bóthar*, a road, as in Stoneybatter. Bishop Street was also the location of the large Jacob's biscuit factory which was occupied by the rebels in the 1916 rising and is now used by the National Archives.

BLACK STREET

Named by the Artisans' Dwellings Company after one of its directors, Gibson Black, who died in 1889.

BLACKHALL PLACE / STREET / PARADE

Named after Sir Thomas Blackhall, Lord Mayor of Dublin in 1769. Originally this area was part of the large expanse of Oxmanstown Green, to which the Normans expelled the Viking residents of Dublin. The area was laid out by Thomas Ivory, who also designed the Law Society building, formerly King's Hospital, otherwise the Blue Coat School. The present building was started in 1773 but was never fully completed. Due to a lack of funds, the intended spire was never built and in the late 19th century, the remains were removed and a small dome placed over the tower. In the 1990s the building was greatly restored. The fine interior contains plasterwork by Charles Thorpe and carvings by Simon Vierpyl. All of the original large red brick houses of Blackhall Street have been removed and replaced with Corporation housing, destroying the intended vista.

BLACKHORSE AVENUE

Previously known as Blackhorse Lane, a name which derived from *The Black Horse* tavern situated here. This was better known to Dubliners as *Nancy Hand's*, from the popular hostess of the pub in the 1800s, or as *The Hole in the Wall* (its official name today) from the turnstile into the adjoining Phoenix Park.

BLACKPITTS

This area was very much involved in the tanning industry, and the name derives from the large vats used to cure the hides. Weaving was also an important industry in the area.

BLESSINGTON STREET

Named after the Earl of Blessington, the eldest son of Luke

Gardiner, who laid out the beginnings of the Gardiner estate on the north side of the city. Other local streets and squares associated with the family name and titles include Gardiner Street and Mountjoy Square. Blessington Street ends at the gates to the former City Basin, now a municipal public park. The basin was developed to supply water to the north of the city, and it also provided water for the two large distilleries, Power's (Thomas Street) and Jameson's (Bow Lane).

BOLTON STREET

Bolton Street is named after the Duke of Bolton, Lord Lieutenant between 1717 and 1721. Together with Dorset Street, it was formerly part of Drumcondra Lane, but it was renamed around 1724 when Henrietta Street was developed. It is now chiefly known as the location of one of the colleges of the Dublin Institute of Technology. This palatial building in red brick and Mountcharles sandstone was designed by the City Architect, Charles J. McCarthy, and built during 1907–12. McCarthy was the son of leading Victorian Gothic architect J. J. McCarthy (1817–82), who was responsible for many churches in Dublin and several Roman Catholic cathedrals around Ireland.

BOND STREET

Named after Oliver Bond (1760–98), a prominent woollen merchant and member of the United Irishmen.

BOW STREET

Formerly Bowes Street but now corrupted to Bow, the street was named after Baron John Bowes, Lord Chancellor of Ireland, who resided here and died in 1767. Originally it was the *Slíghe Mhidhluachra*, one of the four great ancient routes that met in the Dublin area. Now best known as the location of the former Jameson Distillery, it is part of the Smithfield area, which is currently undergoing massive rejuvenation.

BOYNE STREET

Named in 1770, probably to celebrate the Battle of the Boyne (although there is an Erne Street nearby). There was originally a plan to create a Great Boyne Street to lead to the Grand Canal Docks, but this was never completed; interestingly, it is shown on a map of Dublin in 1800.

BRABAZON STREET / PLACE / ROW

Named after Sir Edward Brabazon, Baron of Ardee, whose son was later Earl of Meath. Brabazon Street was originally known as Cuckold's Row.

BRIDE STREET

This is named after St Bride's Church, a pre-Viking foundation, and was first mentioned in 1465 as Synt Bryd Street. The church was demolished in the late 1800s as part of the Iveagh Trust Scheme, the largest single urban renewal project in Edwardian Dublin, which was commissioned by Sir Benjamin Guinness to clean up the slums that surrounded St Patrick's Cathedral, whose restoration he was funding. London architects Joseph, Smitherm and Joseph designed the entire redevelopment scheme, the centrepiece of which was the Iveagh Baths building on Bride Street. A fine example of early art nouveau, this is built of brick set on a granite plinth, and is decorated with terracotta panels. Until its conversion in the 1990s, it contained a fully intact interior entered through a doorway surmounted by a copper-clad dome. The interior has now been much altered, but the exterior survives to be enjoyed.

BRIDGE STREET

Named after the bridge to which it leads, formerly Whitworth Bridge and now Fr Mathew Bridge. There has been a bridge here since the 13th century and the street is mentioned by name as early as 1260. Until the 18th century it reached southwards only as far as Cook Street, but by 1797 it had been extended. The street is the location of Dublin's oldest pub, *The Brazen Head*, to which there are references as far back as 1613. The present building was constructed in 1754 and until comparatively recently was entered through an archway on the street. After street widening, a castellated gateway to the courtyards was erected at the front of the building. Irish revolutionaries to frequent the pub included Robert Emmet, who led the attempted revolt of 1803. It is also incorrectly mentioned by the character Corley in *Ulysses* as 'The Brazen Head over in Winetavern Street'.

BRIDGEFOOT STREET

Derived from the 'Bridge-Foot' – the foot of the bridge. This was also the name of the residence of Sir William Ussher the younger (1610-71), which was situated to the west of Bridge Street and whose grounds occupied the area covered by Usher's Quay and Usher's Island. The street was probably created during the late 17th century to link Thomas Street and what is now Mellowes Bridge. The upper part was previously known as Dirty Lane, and it was only around 1838 that the name was applied to the entire street.

BRITAIN QUAY

Originally Great Britain Quay, it is sited at the end of the long Sir John Rogerson's Quay, and was constructed to allow an entrance to the Grand Canal Docks, opened in 1796.

BROADSTONE

Dominated by the former terminus of the Midland Great Western Railway of 1851, it probably received its name from a stone across the river Bradogue here. The river is now almost totally underground, rising in Cabra and joining the Liffey at Ormond Quay. Broadstone Station is the most monumental of the four railway termini of Dublin, and the only one no longer in use as a railway station. Sited on a hill, its most dramatic feature is the railway shed with its huge colonnade. The station was designed in an austere neo-Egyptian style by John Skipton Mulvany and constructed of granite. The original railway shed roof designed by Richard Turner proved to be too ambitious for the span, and was replaced after it collapsed in the early 1850s. At one stage, a spur of the Royal Canal crossed Phibsborough Road via the Foster Aqueduct to a basin in the forecourt of the station.

BRODIN ROW
Representative of a naming pattern in this area of Stoneybatter based on Norse mythology and history.

BRUNSWICK STREET
Laid out in 1766, this was formerly known as Channel Row, after a channel which connected with the nearby Bradogue River, but it was renamed after the Royal House of Brunswick. It now consists mainly of apartment blocks developed on the site of three of Dublin's most historic hospitals: the Brunswick, the Richmond and the Hardwicke, each of which specialised in a different discipline. The hospitals closed in the 1980s with the opening of Beaumont Hospital near Glasnevin. The former Carmichael School of Medicine (1864) is a fine building in the Lombardesque Revival style, designed by a pupil of Benjamin Woodward.

BUCKINGHAM STREET
Named after the Marquis of Buckingham, Lord Lieutenant in 1782–3 and 1787–90. Buckingham Street contains the earliest of a series of fire stations designed by Charles J. McCarthy, City Architect, which was built in 1899. It is designed in an Italian Romanesque style, with an attached bell tower for sounding the alarm, as at Tara Street. The fire station is now in use as artists' studios.

BULL ALLEY STREET

Like nearby Lamb Alley on the other side of Nicholas Street, Bull Alley probably takes its name from an inn or tavern with the sign of a bull. Designed by the City Architect, C. J. McCarthy, and completed in 1904, the Bull Alley local authority housing scheme was designed to complement the adjacent Iveagh Trust Scheme. These housing blocks are of five storeys surmounted by copper domes over stairwells, with ornate art nouveau details in the gable ends. The ground floors of the buildings were devoted to small shop units, most of which are still in use today.

The dominant building on Bull Alley Street is the Vocational Education College designed in a Flemish Renaissance style by L. A. McDonnell. It is built on what is easily the best site in the Iveagh Trust Scheme, facing cross the park to St Patrick's Cathedral. The park itself was created by Lord Iveagh by removing the existing slums which were built right up to the side of the cathedral. The VEC building has fine stone carving and decoration and was recently restored and cleaned. Although Bull Alley is the name of one street, it has also come to refer to the complete area of housing that takes in Ross Road, Bride Street and Bull Alley itself.

BURGH QUAY

Possibly named after Thomas Burgh, although this is not certain. The name was chosen at a meeting of the Wide Streets Commissioners on 17 May 1805, a meeting at which Burgh, although an active member of the body, was not present. He did however act as chairman at meetings prior to and after this time. It is also possible that the quay was named after Elizabeth Burgh, wife of Anthony Foster, Chief Baron of the Exchequer. Their eldest son was John Foster (1740–1828), the last speaker of the Irish House of Commons. Burgh Quay was best known as the location of the offices of the Irish broadsheet newspaper *The Irish*

Press, which ceased publication in the late 1980s.

BUTT BRIDGE

Named after the MP Sir Isaac Butt (1813–79), founder of the Irish Home Rule movement. Originally from Donegal, Butt was educated at nearby Trinity College and was Professor of Political Economy between 1836 and 1840. Initially opposed to nationalism, Butt was called to the bar in 1838 and developed links with nationalists, defending various people in court, including the Young Irelander William Smith O'Brien. After initially representing Youghal as a Tory MP (1853–65), Butt went on to represent Limerick and led the Home Rule Party in Parliament between 1870 and 1879.

Originally Butt Bridge was a metal swing bridge opened in 1879, which was rotated on a central pier to allow shipping to pass further up the quays. The original bridge was popularly known as the Swivel Bridge and sometimes as the Beresford Swing Bridge. The building of the Loopline railway bridge in 1888 meant that shipping access up the Liffey was now limited, and with its swivelling function no longer required, this part of the bridge remained fixed in a closed position. As early as 1912, proposals were made for the replacement of the bridge because of its narrow width and steep approach gradients. In the 1930s it was rebuilt, becoming the first Liffey bridge to be constructed with reinforced concrete. A photograph exists of the testing of the bridge after construction in 1932, a process that entailed driving a large number of road steam-engines very slowly across the bridge together to create maximum weight.

CAMDEN STREET / PLACE / ROW

Named in 1778 – but not as supposed after Lord Camden, who did not become Lord Lieutenant until 1795. With its very elaborate Edwardian shop interior, Carvill's off-licence at No. 39 Camden Street remained open for business until very recently. Its features included a curvilinear manager's cubicle to ensure constant supervision of staff at the shop counter. Also worthy of note in the street is the fine exterior of the Bleeding Horse public house, with its large windows and cast iron supports. Unfortunately, the original interior is long gone. *The Bleeding Horse*, originally founded in 1648, is famously mentioned in the works of Seán O'Casey and was frequented by both James Clarence Mangan and Joseph Sheridan Le Fanu, who gives a good description of the previous building to the current Victorian façade:

> 'There stood at the southern extremity of the city, near the point at which Camden Street now terminates, a small, old-fashioned building, something between an alehouse and an inn. It occupied the roadside by no means unpicturesquely; one gable fitted into the road, with a projecting window, which stood out from the building like a glass box held together by a massive frame of wood; and commanded by this projecting gable; and a few yards in retreat, but facing the road, was the inn door, over which hung a painted panel, representing a white horse, out of whose neck there sprouted a crimson cascade and underneath, in large letters, the traveler [*sic*] was informed that this was the genuine old Bleeding Horse.'

CAPEL STREET

Named after the family of the Lord Lieutenant of 1672–7, Lord Arthur Capel, Earl of Essex. The street was laid out by a property developer, Sir Humphrey Jervis, on the lands of St Mary's Abbey, which he purchased around 1674. He promised Essex that he would lay out a street and name it after him in acknowledgment of his assistance with his developments. Essex went on to become First Lord of the Treasury in England, and was later accused of conspiring with the Duke of Monmouth against Charles II in 1682. He was imprisoned in the Tower of London and was later found with his throat cut.

CARDIFF LANE

Originally Cardiff's Lane after Mathew Cardiff who had boatyards here behind the quay walls constructed by Sir John Rogerson when the area was still largely open countryside.

CARLINGFORD PARADE

Named after the town in Co. Louth.

CARLISLE STREET

Possibly named after the Earl of Carlisle, Lord Lieutenant in 1780-82.

CARMAN'S HALL

According to Rocque's map of 1756 this was Cammon Hall, called after the tavern from which the coaches left for Wexford. Possibly transformed into 'Carman', meaning coachman, because of this.

CASTLE STEPS

Previously known as Cole's Alley due to a tavern, *The Royal Chop House* owned by a Mr Cole, this passage, which is gated at both ends, contains a steep flight of steps connecting Castle Street and Little Ship Street.

CASTLE STREET

So named because prior to the construction of Lord Edward Street it was the main route to Dublin Castle. Running alongside the castle walls, the street has largely been rebuilt in recent years.

Dublin Castle was founded in 1204 by order of King John who wanted a fortress constructed for the administration of the city. The castle was placed on high ground to the east of the city, and was originally protected by the Poddle river (now flowing underground) which was later used to fill a moat around the walls. In 1224 the castle was provided with a chapel.

Up until the 15th century Dublin Castle's role was mainly administrative, concerned with setting up the machinery of government rather than with defence. In 1534, however, it was subjected to siege by Thomas Fitzgerald, better known as Silken Thomas. At the Council of State gathering at St Mary's Abbey, Silken Thomas renounced his allegiance to King Henry VIII in the belief that his father, the Earl of Kildare, had been executed in London. His attack on the castle came from one side only and was easily defended, and when the populace heard that the King was sending troops, they turned on the attackers, who laid siege to the city in retaliation. Fitzgerald was later captured and executed in London along with five uncles.

The castle at this time occupied roughly the area of the current upper yard, with one entrance and some fortified towers. By the beginning of the 17th century it was fully developed, housing law courts, meetings of Parliament, the residence of the Viceroy and a council chamber. This was a violent period in which many attempts were made to capture the castle. Like the city wall, it originally had an area free of buildings immediately beyond the perimeter to allow for easier defence, but as the years passed and the city developed this was filled in, leaving the castle more vulnerable. The main danger however arose not from without but within. On 7 April 1684 a fire broke out in the viceregal quarters. In order to prevent the fire from spreading from here to the Powder Tower, some of the buildings in between were blown up, and the castle ceased to have the form of a medieval fortress.

New designs by the Surveyor General Sir William Robinson were completed by October 1688. The buildings are clearly of the same lineage as the Royal Hospital Kilmainham, which Robinson also designed, with a similar ground-floor arcade and steep, dormered roofline. The block linking the two coachyards had three coach arches in the centre to allow access from one to the other, although the yards also had their own separate exits to the city beyond the walls. In the 18th century as the Georgian streetscape of Dublin was being developed, the castle too underwent significant change. A young architect, believed to be Sir Edward Lovett Pearce, redesigned the upper yard using the basic design inherited from Sir William Robinson. These ranges constructed in the 1680s are similar in plan and placement to those present today.

The Genealogical Office or Bedford Tower was constructed around the 1750s, along with its two flanking gateways to the city. The clock tower was named after the Duke of Bedford and Lord Lieutenant of Ireland, John Russell, and is constructed on the site of one of the original towers. The state apartments for the Viceroy were built during this period (although an attic storey was constructed in place of the dormers in the 19th century), and the upper yard was laid out as it exists today. In 1779 it was stated that 'this castle is far superior to the palace of St James's as well as in the exterior, as to the size and elegance of the apartments within'. During the rebellion of 1798, the courtyard was used for storing the dead and wounded – a fate never endured by St James's. The rising led by Robert Emmet resulted in 1803 in another failed attempt to capture the castle.

Throughout the 19th century Dublin Castle remained the centre of British rule in Ireland, and even during the Famine the balls, receptions and dinners continued. In 1916 the castle came under its last attack, which it also survived. It remained in the hands of the British authorities until it was handed over to the Free State on 16 January 1922. One of the most infamous events in its 20th century history occurred in 1907 when the Irish Crown Jewels were stolen from the Bedford Tower. This incident took place only the day before a visit by the King and Queen in one of the most heavily fortified areas in either Britain or Ireland. Neither jewels nor thief were ever discovered.

The castle is still used for state occasions such as presidential inaugurations, and it was the centre of much activity during the period of Ireland's presidency of the European Union in 1990. During renovations in the 1980s it was deemed necessary to rebuild the foundations beneath the lower yard. In the process the remains of the city wall were discovered, along with one of the city gates and one of the original castle towers. Also found was the junction where the Poddle river (now subterranean) was used to feed the castle moat running under the walls.

No. 4 Castle Street has been restored by the Dublin Civic Trust as its headquarters and an exhibition space, while the Rates Office frames the other end of this street with City Hall. The Rates Office, a fine tall building on a good site facing down Cork Hill, was originally built as the Newcomen Bank by Thomas Ivory in 1781. The extension (1858) added by the Hibernian Bank after the failure of the Newcomen Bank simply mirrored the design of the original building, the join masked by a curved columned porch. When Lord Edward Street was completed the rear elevation was remodelled and the fountain added in 1881.

The history of the Newcomen Bank is a complex one. In 1722 William Gleadowe married into the Newcomen family of Carriglass in County Longford and assumed the Newcomen name. In 1781 he was knighted and elected to the Irish Parliament. He voted in favour of the Act of Union, and as a reward his wife was granted a peerage – an event that resulted in many verses and songs (none of them complimentary) about the family. On his father's death in 1807 Thomas Viscount Newcomen inherited the bank, together with his mother's title. The bank closed in 1825 after a series of banking failures in the city during that decade. With the bank's collapse and his family's ruination, Newcomen shot himself in his office, aged forty-eight. As he had not married, the title became extinct after his death.

CASTLEFORBES ROAD

Part of the North Lotts area on the North Wall, Castleforbes Road is named after a building on Upper Sheriff Street that was inscribed with the date 1729 and called Castle Forbes. Perhaps the builder of this relic of the early days of the Hanoverian succession was George Forbes, who was Lord Mayor in 1720. Formerly known as Fish Street.

CATHAL BRUGHA STREET

Originally Gregg Lane but renamed after one of the protagonists of the 1916 rising during the reconstruction of the O'Connell Street area in the 1920s. Severely wounded during the rising, Cathal Brugha (1874–1922) was a leading republican who presided over the first meeting of Dáil Éireann in the Mansion House in 1919. He became the first Minister for Defence. Opposed to the Treaty, he was killed early in the Civil War.

CATHEDRAL LANE

Located just off Kevin Street, this was originally Cabbage Garden Lane, but since 1792 it has been known as Cathedral Lane because of its proximity to St Patrick's Cathedral. In 1649 Cromwell ordered cabbages to be planted here to provide green vegetables for his soldiers. In 1685 the Archbishop of Dublin allocated a 150-foot strip of the garden to French Huguenots to use as a burial ground, which they continued to do until 1858.

CATHEDRAL STREET

While there are two Church of Ireland cathedrals in Dublin, no Roman Catholic cathedral exists. This street was optimistically named for its proximity to (Catholic) St Mary's Pro-Cathedral, opened in 1825. The design was the result of an architectural competition awarded to John Sweetman, but it has never been known for certain if it was truly his. Sweetman had been exiled in Paris as a result of his participation in the rebellion of 1798. A theory exists that it may in fact have been a leading French architect of the day, Louis Hippolyte Le Bas, who was responsible for the Pro-Cathedral's design, since the interior closely resembles a church designed by him in Paris, while the exterior is similar to that of another Parisian church, completed in 1824. It is possible that during his stay in Paris Sweetman may have had contact with Le Bas with a view to entering the competition.

CATHERINE STREET

Named after the Parish of St Catherine and the two nearby churches bearing the same name – the Roman Catholic church on Meath Street, and the former Church of Ireland church on Thomas Street.

CECILIA STREET

Named after a member of the Fownes family who developed Cope Street and Fownes Street. It is also possible that it was named after Saint Cecilia as it was called 'S. Cecelia Street' in maps from 1798.

CHAMBER STREET

The Brabazons, Earls of Meath, owned most of this area, and the street is named after the Chambre family of Stormanstown (Co. Louth), with whom they intermarried around 1680.

CHAMPIONS AVENUE

Dublin Corporation housing development opened in the 1980s

and named after the many boxing champions who lived in the area in the 1930s.

CHANCERY LANE
So called because of the many Chancery lawyers who lived here in the 18th century when the Examiner's Office of the Court of Chancery was in nearby Darby Square. Once reached via a passageway off Werburgh Street, the square no longer exists.

CHANCERY PLACE
Named for its proximity to the Court of Chancery, one of the four courts. Also called Lucy Lane and Mass Lane because of the Jesuit Church that was here until 1687. This later became a Huguenot chapel. Part of the street was also known as Mountrath Street after Charles Coote, Earl of Mountrath (died 1661).

CHANCERY STREET
Located behind the buildings housing the four courts and named after one of them, the Court of Chancery. Before the Four Courts was constructed the street was Pill Lane (later Pill Street) having been built on the inlet known as the Pill, on which St Mary's Abbey had a small harbour. The name was changed to Chancery Street in the 1890s.

CHARLEMONT BRIDGE
Named after Charlemont Street, which meets the Grand Canal here.

CHARLEMONT STREET / PARADE / MALL
Named after James Caulfield (1728–9), first Earl of Charlemont and Commander-in-Chief of the Irish Volunteers in 1780. Charlemont was a connoisseur of the arts, over-stretching his income to build Charlemont House on Rutland (now Parnell) Square, as well as the Casino at Marino, designed by Sir William

Chambers (1723–96). Charlemont Street was the site of an ambitious public housing scheme undertaken in the 1930s, of which only a small part was ever built. Ffrench-Mullan House was designed by the architect Michael Scott (1905–89).

CHARLES STREET, GREAT
Named after Charles Coote (died 1661), who established a successful planter army in Sligo and Leitrim and was Lord President of Connacht in 1645. In 1660 he was an important figure in the restoration of Charles II, who rewarded him with lands and the title of Earl of Mountrath. There was also a Mountrath Street nearby, but this is now part of Chancery Place.

CHARLEVILLE MALL
Both this street and nearby Charleville Avenue, formerly Bayview Parade, seem to have had some association with the family of Bury, Earls of Charleville, a title that became extinct in 1875.

CHARLOTTE QUAY / STREET/ WAY
These are all named after Queen Charlotte (1744–1818), wife of King George III. Charlotte Quay bounds the southern side of the larger basin of the Grand Canal Docks. Charlotte Way was a new street opened to link Camden Street and Harcourt Street after office development in the early 1990s eliminated the old right of way known as Old Camden Street.

CHATHAM STREET
Named after William Pitt (1759–1806), son of the first Earl of Chatham. Neighbouring Balfe Street was once known as Pitt Street.

CHESTERFIELD AVENUE
The main avenue through the Phoenix Park from Parkgate Street to Castleknock Gates. It is named after Lord Chesterfield, Lord

Lieutenant in 1744–7, who was responsible for reopening the park to the public after it had for a time been the private preserve of the viceregal lodge (now Áras an Uachtaráin).

CHRISTCHURCH PLACE

Named after Christ Church Cathedral, this was formerly known as Skinners' Row as it was the centre of the skinning industry in medieval Dublin. Prior to this, it was known as Bothe Street. Nearby High Street was also an important centre for the leather trade. In the 17th and 18th centuries the Tholsel or city hall was sited in Skinners' Row. In 1821, this narrow street, then only twelve feet wide, was expanded to its current width and renamed Christchurch Place.

Christ Church Cathedral is the Church of Ireland cathedral for the diocese of Dublin and Glendalough. Its history goes back to about 1030, when the Viking settlers constructed a church on this site. The present building dates to 1172 when Archbishop Laurence O'Toole and the Norman knight Richard de Clare – known as Strongbow – initiated the building work. Following European tradition, the canons of the cathedral were monks, the Canons Regular of St Augustine. When the Church in England broke away from Rome, the majority of the Irish bishops followed suit, and the last of the Augustinian priors became the first Dean of Christ Church.

Throughout the years, Christ Church has undergone a number of restorations: in 1358, 1562, 1829 and again in 1871. Because of the extensive restorations and renovations carried out in the 1870s by the English architect George Edward Street, the cathedral as it exists today is mainly Victorian. This work of restoration cost over £230,000, and like the renovations at nearby St Patrick's Cathedral it was funded by a member of a brewing family, the whiskey distiller Henry Roe, who generously covered the entire cost, just as Benjamin Guinness had done with St Patrick's. Up until the 1700s houses were built right up to the cathedral on all sides, and it was not until Street's restoration that the grounds were cleared to allow an unobstructed view.

Externally the cathedral seems to wander all over the hillside. After initial completion the building was extended lengthwise rather than upwards. In the grounds are the remains of a chapter house dating from the time when this was a monastery church. The original long choir was removed in the 1870s by Street. The cathedral is linked to the Synod Hall by an enclosed bridge across Winetavern Street. Originally this was a separate church, St Michael's, which was only connected to the main cathedral in the 1870s. The most interesting external feature of Christ Church is the fine Romanesque doorway in the gable of the southern transept. This original doorway, dating from the 12th century, is one of the external features not 'restored' or replaced by Street. The interior is mainly Victorian, dating from the restoration.

The crypt of Christ Church, dating from 1188, is the oldest surviving part of the building and is one of the largest medieval crypts in Britain and Ireland. At 175 feet long it stretches the length of the building, with a maze of huge stone columns supporting the cathedral above. Many historic pieces of stonework and fittings are stored here, including the statues from the top of the old Tholsel (the city hall) and the stocks. After the demolition of the Tholsel, the statues of Charles I and Charles II and the Stuart coats-of-arms were moved here. The stocks, made in 1670, were previously kept in Christ Church yard but were moved here in 1870. Many pieces of stonework removed and replaced during George Street's restoration are also kept here, including monuments to important families and carved stones from the demolished long choir.

CHURCH LANE
So called because it led from the Houses of Parliament on College

Green to St Andrews Church, which served as Parliament's chapel. One side of this narrow street is occupied by the National Irish Bank; the other by O'Neill's public house, a fine half-timbered building with a corbelled, gabled, oriel window designed by G. P. Sheridan in 1908.

CHURCH STREET

Named after the church of St Michan the Martyr, first dedicated in 1095. The present structure dates from 1685–6, and was built on the site of the earlier one founded by the Norse. Originally St Michan's was built to serve the Viking community that had been expelled from the walled city after the Normans became a dominant power in Dublin. For almost five hundred years this was the only parish church on the north side of the Liffey. It may have been designed by Sir William Robinson, architect of the Royal Hospital Kilmainham, and it was rebuilt when Sir Humphrey Jervis redeveloped the area. The church contains one of the oldest organs still in use in this country, which Handel is believed to have played on while finishing *Messiah*. The church however is more famous for its collection of mummified bodies stored in the vaults. The limestone in the ground keeps the air dry and assists in the process of preservation. Many of the leaders of the 1798 rebellion are buried in the vaults and surrounding graveyard.

Also in Church Street is the Roman Catholic church of St Mary of the Angels, which opened in 1881. It was designed by the leading church architect J. J. McCarthy, who died before it was completed. Money originally intended for a tower and spire was then used to provide a presbytery and other accommodation. McCarthy's son, C. J. McCarthy, City Architect, designed the Corporation housing built across the street.

CITY QUAY

In 1715 the City Corporation took over the project of connecting a wall already completed at Hawkins Street (then Hawkins Quay) to Sir John Rogerson's Quay, soon to be constructed. The work was originally to be undertaken by John Mercer, who had built Mercer's Dock at Poolbeg Street, but by 1712 it was apparent that he was not going to complete the task. Rocque's map of 1756 makes no mention of City Quay and shows Sir John Rogerson Quay directly linked to George's Quay. This suggests that the name evolved rather than being formally applied upon completion of the building work.

CLANBRASSIL STREET

Named after James Hamilton (1729–98), second Earl of Clanbrassil, one of the founder members of the Royal Irish Academy. No. 52 Upper Clanbrassil Street was the 'birthplace' in May 1866 of the character Leopold Bloom in James Joyce's *Ulysses*.

CLANWILLIAM PLACE

Named after the third Earl of Clanwilliam, who married into the Pembroke estate through an alliance with Elizabeth Herbert, daughter of the Eleventh Earl of Pembroke.

CLARE STREET

Named after Denzille Holles (1597–1681), Earl of Clare (in Suffolk, not Ireland). For a time Samuel Beckett (1906–89) lived on the top floor of No. 6 above the offices of his father's firm. It was here that he wrote his first novel *More Pricks than Kicks*, and much of his later work, including *Murphy*.

CLARENCE MANGAN ROAD

Named after the poet James Clarence Mangan (1803–49), who was born in Fishamble Street and died of malnutrition in the Meath Hospital. Mangan's birthplace was demolished in 1944 and the *Castle Inn* now occupies the site. Mangan lived most of his life in poverty. His poetry was published in many journals and magazines, but he is best known for songs and ballads such as 'Dark Rosaleen'.

CLARENCE STREET
Named after the Duke of Clarence, William IV (1765–1837).

CLARENDON STREET / ROW
Named after Henry Hyde, second Earl of Clarendon (1638–1709), one of the Wide Streets Commissioners and Lord Lieutenant in 1685. Like nearby William Street, Clarendon Street was developed by the brewer and property developer William Williams on land that was once part of the monastery of All Hallows.

CLARKE'S BRIDGE
Crossing the Royal Canal at Ballybough, this was named after Edward Clarke, a director of the Royal Canal Company in 1791.

CLONMEL STREET
Named after John Scott, Baron Earlsfort and Earl of Clonmell (1739–98). (Like other earls whose titles ended in the letter l, Scott added a second one.) His home, Clonmell House, was at 16–17 Harcourt Street and faced Clonmel Street. He also owned the extensive pleasure grounds – now Iveagh Gardens – lying between Harcourt Street, Clonmel Street and Earlsfort Terrace. The street today is a pleasant cul-de-sac leading to the gardens.

CLYDE ROAD
Named after the soldier Sir Colin Campbell, later Lord Clyde (1792–1863), who relieved Lucknow in India during the 1857 Mutiny.

COBURG PLACE
Coburg Place (1822), like Coburg Gardens (now the beautiful and extensive Iveagh Gardens off Harcourt Street), takes its name

from the family of Saxe Coburg to which both the mother and the husband of Queen Victoria belonged. Princess Charlotte, only child of George IV, was married in 1816 to Prince Leopold of Coburg.

COGHILL'S COURT

A narrow opening off Dame Street now leading to the side entrance of the Irish Film Centre. It was named in 1766 after Sir John Coghill, who died in 1699 and was a Master in Chancery.

COLERAINE STREET

Like several of the streets that surround it, this was named because of its proximity to the Linen Hall after one of the principal towns involved in the linen trade in Ulster.

COLLEGE GREEN

Named after Trinity College in the 1600s but originally known as Hoggen Green, deriving from the Scandinavian word for mound. The nearby nunnery of the Blessed Virgin Mary del Hogges was founded in 1156. Also in the area was the Thingmote, the Viking place of assembly. College Green is something of a misnomer nowadays, as this is a very busy thoroughfare for traffic and pedestrians and the only grass visible is inside the railings of Trinity College.

Trinity College has one of the finest façades in the city, dominating College Green along with the former Houses of Parliament, now the Bank of Ireland. In 1751 the board of the college asked Parliament for financial help in reconstructing the main buildings. Trinity had close links with Parliament, having two Members of its own, and anyone wearing a college gown had the automatic right of entry to debates in the House of Commons (a privilege revoked by Speaker Foster in 1795). As any unspent money was returned to the English Parliament, Irish MPs were very receptive to the idea of spending all their money in Dublin, and the finance for the reconstruction work was made available.

The result was that the college was housed more grandly than any in Cambridge or Oxford. Originally the 150-foot long frontage, designed by the English amateur architect Theodore Jacobsen, was to be crowned with three copper cupolas, one at either end and a massive one in the centre. These plans were disrupted when a traveller recently returned from Europe – obviously a person with political clout – objected to the cupolas on the grounds that they were 'no where to be met with in Italy in such buildings'. The construction of the cupola on the north side had already begun, and until recently its traces could be seen from above. The massive vaulting for the central cupola still exists at ground level.

The external design was used in a modified, plainer form in the quadrangle known as Parliament Square in recognition of the munificence that allowed it to be built. William Chambers, who designed the chapel and the examination hall, originally wanted Parliament Square to be completed with a range of monumental buildings in the area of the present Campanile. Their absence has left the square open at one end when viewed from the west, without the sense of a quadrangle or of 'monumentality'. From the east however one can imagine the square as Chambers intended it.

Across from Trinity College are the former Houses of Parliament, the first purpose-built parliament house in the world, constructed at a time of great public confidence in Dublin. The original building is only a part of the existing structure – the central section with its huge colonnades. It was designed by Edward Lovett Pearce (1699–1733) and constructed between 1729 and 1739. Pearce received a knighthood in the building on 10 March 1731. The east and west porticos were designed by James Gandon (1743–1823) between 1785 and 1797, and the curving screen walls were added by Francis Johnston (1760–1829) when the building was being converted to a bank in 1803. Like other buildings in Dublin, notably the Custom House, the Bank of Ireland is graced by sculptures by Edward Smyth (1743–1823). These are in place over the portico to the House of Lords and symbolise Wisdom, Justice and Liberty.

Parliament in the 18th century was largely controlled by the wealthy ascendancy. On 2 August 1800 it was persuaded to vote itself out of existence through the Act of Union. Many landlords and members of the Irish aristocracy were swayed by promises of titles and honours from London. With the Act of Union, the centre of power shifted to the English capital, and many of the ascendancy moved to London when not living on their country estates. After this, Dublin began a slow slide into a state of disrepair. The famous Gardiner estate went bankrupt, and many of the glorious Georgian streets fell into decay as the houses were split up into tenements. The parliament building was sold to the Bank of Ireland under the condition that it should not be used for political assemblies.

The Parliament had consisted of two houses, the House of Commons and the House of Lords. The Commons is now the banking hall, while the Lords remains intact. The interiors designed by Pearce have survived except for the original Commons, destroyed by fire in 1792. The most immediate impression is that presented by the coffered ceiling and oak panelling. Two tapestries by John van Beaver depict the Battle of the Boyne. The remainder of the interior dates from Francis Johnston's reconstruction. The House of Lords occupied a less important position than the Commons, and is situated off the main axis to the left. It has survived and is open to the public. It is reached by passing from Gandon's great portico to the east through a processional series of rooms and corridors. The corridors that wind around the original site of the House of Commons are illuminated by small domes lit from above.

There are many statues and sculptures in College Green, including those of Goldsmith and Burke inside the railings of Trinity College. A statue of Henry Grattan faces the scene of the many debates in which he participated, while one of Thomas Davis, together with a fountain, was added in 1966. Like Dame Street, College Green has many fine 19th century buildings housing banks and financial institutions.

COLLEGE STREET

A short street flanking Trinity College, from which the name derives. At one time it was intended to construct an entrance to the college here, opposite the end of D'Olier Street, with a suitable frontage to complete the Georgian vista from Drogheda Street (now incorporated into O'Connell Street) down D'Olier Street. For a brief period after 1821 College Street was known as Bank Street, reflecting the Bank of Ireland's installation in the former Houses of Parliament on College Green. Its former name was restored in 1835.

College Street contains one of Dublin's finest bank buildings, designed in 1863 as the headquarters of the Provincial Bank and now part of a new hotel development. The cost of the building ran to twice the original estimate, and the architect, William Murray, died in dispute with the bank over his fees. The design comprises a seven-bay main building over three storeys, with a pompous pediment and columns. The pediment relief sculptures are by S. F. Lynn and depict banking, agriculture attended by farm workers, the labour force depicted by a servant and produce personified in an African man. To the rear, on Fleet Street, is an office block with round-topped windows. A magnificent central banking hall was constructed, but unfortunately no funds remained to provide the bank's directors and management with similar accommodation at first floor level. Also, as the site was an irregular shape the banking hall is in fact off-centre.

COMMONS STREET

Part of a naming pattern in this part of the North Lotts reflecting institutions of power and important civic functions. Also in the area are Sheriff Street, Mayor Street and Guild Street.

CONSTITUTION HILL

So named because of its proximity to the King's Inns. Previously known as Glasmanogue and North Townsend Street. The area is dominated by the King's Inns, the last great public building designed by James Gandon, which was created to provide study and residence facilities for barristers. As with the Four Courts, the building process was plagued by delays. Having begun in 1795, Gandon resigned from the job in 1808 and handed the project over to his pupil, Henry Aaron Baker, who finished the work in 1816. Like the Four Courts and the Custom House, the building was designed with its main western façade on a waterfront, the Royal Canal having once had a spur and harbour where the park is now. Originally there was also a plan for a crescent, to contain barristers' chambers, but this was never constructed.

Like Gandon's other creations, the building has a copper dome which is positioned centrally on the symmetrical composition. The use of copper-clad domes, which Gandon popularised in Dublin, is a very Scandinavian motif. In France and England domes were usually clad in lead, giving them a grey appearance. The building also reflects Gandon's dislike of windows, and it has many blank niches breaking up the building's surface. The two entrance blocks project from the main accommodation and contain the Registry of Deeds and the dining hall. Each of the two entrances has caryatides (female figures used as pillars) by Edward Smyth supporting the cornices on either side. Those at the doorway to the Registry of Deeds represent Security and Law. One of the pair at the entrance to the dining hall represents Plenty; the other is a 'Bacchante' or priestess of Bacchus, the Greek and Roman god of wine.

CONYNGHAM ROAD

Named after the first Marquis of Conyngham, one of the Wide Street Commissioners, who partly funded its construction in 1786. It was previously known as the Way to Islandbridge.

COOK STREET

Named after the guild of cooks which was based here in medieval times. Also known as Le Coke Street or Vicus Cocorom. What are considered to be the two remaining stretches of the city wall visible above ground can be seen on Cook Street at St Audoen's Church and at the nearby Cornmarket, although in recent years portions of the wall, gates and towers have been uncovered during excavations for new buildings in the quay areas and in Temple Bar. A building demolished in the early 1990s on Wellington Quay was found to have a very thick rear wall. It is now assumed that this was a portion of the original city wall and that the house was built up against it in the early 1700s. Excavation of the site later revealed the foundations of one of the city wall's towers. This area was the site of one of the original river crossings of the old city, and gates and towers were erected for its protection. The sole surviving city gate is visible at St Audoen's and leads to a narrow alley around the side of the church. Known as St Audoen's Gate, it was one of the main entrances to the medieval city.

THE COOMBE

The name in Irish, an Cúm, means a hollow place. The Coombe gave its name to the well-known Dublin maternity hospital founded here by a wealthy widow in 1826, in a building occupied by the Meath Hospital before the latter moved to Long Lane. The maternity hospital transferred to a new building in Cork Street in 1967.

COPE STREET

Named after Robert Cope, who married Elizabeth Fownes, a

member of the Fownes family who owned land here and gave its name to neighbouring Fownes Street.

COPPER ALLEY

Previously known as Preston's Inns and renamed in 1705 after the copper money coined and distributed here in 1608 by Lady Alice Fenton, widow of the Secretary of State in Ireland, Sir Geoffrey Fenton. A long, narrow, dingy laneway, this has recently been redeveloped by Temple Bar Properties to create a new link with Essex Street, allowing the former Church of St John the Evangelist to close the vista.

COPPINGER'S ROW

A narrow street running alongside the Powerscourt Townhouse Centre, named after Robert Coppinger of neighbouring William Street.

CORK HILL

Named after the first Earl of Cork, Richard Boyle, whose home, Cork House, was built around 1600 on the site of the demolished church of Sainte Marie del Dam, now occupied by City Hall. The church and nearby Dame Street owe their names to the dam or mill pond that once existed in the area.

After Richard Boyle's death, Cork House was used for government offices and other purposes, including that of Cromwell's headquarters in Ireland. At one point in the 1750s it was proposed that a square be constructed here to be known as Bedford Square, after the Lord Lieutenant, the Duke of Bedford. Instead, the site was acquired by the city at a cost of £13,000 for use as a Royal Exchange. In 1768 architects were invited to submit designs for the building. Sixty-one designs in all were received and were exhibited in William Street Exhibition Room. After consideration, the first prize was awarded to Thomas Cooley, a young architect new to Dublin. James Gandon came second with a design that many thought superior. Cooley did not live long enough to build on this success after its completion, for he died five years later in 1784. (Gandon may be said to have had his revenge, for upon Cooley's death, as architect of the Four Courts, he amalgamated Cooley's design for a Public Records Office into his own complex as the western block.)

The new Exchange building was started promptly after the competition and was completed in 1779 at a cost of £40,000, raised through lotteries. The building is set on a slope on a rusticated pedestal with a balustrade. With its giant portico and copper dome, it dominates and completes the view from Capel Street up through Parliament Street. The two main façades to the north and west are similar, while the eastern façade, which faced onto a narrow lane, received plainer treatment. With the demolition of buildings on Dame Street in the 20th century, this façade is now visible across a small park built by the Corporation on the derelict site. The pedimented façades have a giant order of Corinthian columns with three openings between them. The entire ground floor was originally one space divided only by the columns that support the great dome. The doorways led directly in to this open space. The placing of the external columns and pilasters reflects the positioning of the internal columns. The upper floor was reached by two oval staircases at each corner of the north side of the interior. At the top of these stairs was a room used as a coffee room by the city merchants. A contemporary report describes the interior thus:

> 'The dome is spacious, lofty and noble, and is supported by twelve composite fluted columns, which, rising from the floor, form a circular walk in the centre of the ambulatory; the entablature over the columns is enriched in the most splendid manner, and above that are twelve elegant circular windows. The ceiling of the dome is decorated with stucco ornaments in

the mosaic taste, divided into small hexagonal compartments, and in the centre is a large window, which lights most of the building.'

In 1852 the building was acquired by the City Corporation. Changes were made internally, with screen walls added to the large entrance hall, thus forming the rotunda. This massive entrance rotunda now dominates the interior, with the Corporation's elaborate seal set into the floor mosaic. Its authoritarian motto, 'Obedientia Civium Urbis Felicitas' translates roughly as 'Happy the city where citizens obey.' The subdivision of the ground floor has had the effect of emphasising the rotunda and its top-lit dome. Unlike those of the Four Courts and the Custom House, the interiors of this building are intact as originally designed, save for the alterations carried out in 1852 which were happily removed in 2000. It is now the meeting place of the city aldermen, and the coffee room has become the chamber of the City Council.

Thomas John Barnardo (1845–1905), the founder of Barnardo's Homes, was born in Cork Hill. The house no longer exists but a plaque commemorates him in the small park alongside City Hall.

CORK STREET

Named after the first Earl of Cork. In ancient times, it was the *Slíghe Dála*, one of the great roads across Ireland that met at the Liffey. It was intended to widen Cork Street into a dual carriageway but that plan has now been dropped. It did, however, cause the street to fall into decay, as the threat of a compulsory purchase order did not encourage property owners to invest in the area.

CORN EXCHANGE PLACE

In Rocque's map of 1756, this was White's Lane, but it was renamed following the building of the Corn Exchange on Burgh Quay in the mid-19th century. The Corn Exchange may have been designed by George Halpin, Inspector of Works for the Ballast Board. It had an imposing stone façade on Burgh Quay, with a market hall on the Poolbeg Street side of the building.

CORNMARKET

According to Walter Harris's *History and Antiquities of Dublin* (the first major history of the city, published in 1766), this was previously known as 'New-gate-street', but it has been called by its present name since the early 17th century. This was where corn was traded until recent years, when the market was removed to Thomas Street and a spacious and convenient edifice erected for the purpose. The Corn Market still retains its name, although it is now chiefly employed as a market for coarse linens. At one time, there were many lanes leading from what is now Cornmarket and High Street down to Cook Street. One of these narrow laneways, Keyser's Lane, was the scene of a riot in 1496 at which the Mayor of Dublin, Jenico Marks, was killed. In later years, it became known in popular parlance as Kiss-arse Lane because it was so steep and slippery that those who went down it unwarily were often subject to falls.

CORPORATION STREET

Part of a series of streets named after institutions of power in this area of the North Lotts. Originally named Mabbot Street after Gilbert Mabbot, who had a water mill that stood here until around 1715. The street was renamed in the early part of the 20th century.

COWPER STREET

In 1874 all the Gardiner property in Dublin, with the exception of Henrietta Street, was sold in one lot for £120,000 to the Honourable Charles Spencer Cowper, son-in-law of Lord Blessington.

CRAMPTON QUAY
Named after the Lord Mayor in 1758, Philip Crampton (1696–1792). The Cramptons were important landowners in the Temple Bar area.

CRANE LANE
So named because of the public crane erected nearby in 1571 beside the old Custom House, close to the site of the Clarence Hotel. A previous crane had been put in place by the Normans here in the 13th century. The first synagogue in Dublin was possibly in Crane Lane in 1663.

CREIGHTON STREET
From the family name of Abraham Creighton, the first Lord Erne, who acquired property in this area through marriage to the daughter of Sir John Rogerson. The street may have been known as Ordnance Lane prior to 1800.

CROMWELL'S QUARTERS
Like nearby Roundhead Row, this was renamed by the Corporation in 1876. It was known previously by the uninviting name of Murdering Lane. While Cromwell did stop over in Dublin with a large garrison in 1649, he lodged at the corner of Werburgh Street and Castle Street and there does not seem to be any particular link with this area. It is likely that the street was simply renamed along with Roundhead Row as part of a themed naming pattern.

CROSS GUNS BRIDGE
Spanning the Grand Canal near Phibsborough, it was named after an inn or tavern with a sign that showed crossed guns.

CROWE STREET
Named after William Crowe, who was granted a medieval

mansion and garden in this area in 1597. His home was known as the 'Crowe's Nest', and later housed various government departments. In 1684 the Dublin Society established a botanic garden and laboratory here. Crowe Street also gave its name in the 18th century to the famous Crowe Street Theatre, opened in opposition to another well-known establishment, the Smock Alley Theatre. In 1836 a medical school was erected on the same site, which was sold to the Catholic University of Ireland in 1855 and operated until the 1930s. The building still exists as Cecilia House.

CROWN ALLEY
Narrow Crown Alley leads from Temple Bar through Merchant's Arch to the quays, and was probably named after a tavern which stood here.

CUFFE STREET
Named after Sir James Cuffe, husband of Alice Aungier, whose family owned property in this area and was responsible for developing Aungier Street and Longford Street. It is referred to in Rocque's map of 1756 as Great Cuffe Street, with Mercer Street Upper shown as Little Cuffe Street. The street was widened in the 1970s to provide a dual carriageway for traffic to St Stephen's Green.

CUMBERLAND STREET NORTH / SOUTH
Named after William Augustus (1721–65), Duke of Cumberland and son of King George II. Richard Crosbie – the first Irish person to achieve flight by ascending from Leinster Lawn in a balloon on 19 July 1765 – lived in Cumberland Street North, which had been laid out some decades previously. Cumberland Street South was shown on Rocque's map of 1756 as a country laneway.

CURVED STREET

This is one of Dublin's newest streets, the last link in the pedestrian route from Temple Bar Square to Meetinghouse Square. The street is formed by the two buildings facing onto it, Arthouse Multimedia Centre and the Music Centre, and it is curved – hence the rather unimaginative name. Arthouse is a complex of four storeys over basement occupying the concave side of the street. It houses a multimedia arts centre and a cyber café. The central part of the building's façade is glazed to allow natural light from the central atrium to light the street, which would otherwise be totally in shadow. Openings of differing sizes puncture the curved façade, with the largest panel opening for access. There is also a top floor terrace.

CURZON STREET

A small street of Victorian houses off the South Circular Road. It is named after George Nathaniel Curzon (1859–1925), first Marquis of Kedleston, perhaps the most important British statesman of the modern era not to become Prime Minister. A statesman, historian, and traveller, Curzon was seen as a political figure who achieved 'successes rather than success'. After distinctions at Eton and Oxford, he became Private Secretary in 1885 to the new Prime Minister, Lord Salisbury. In 1886, he was elected to the House of Commons. Posts as Under Secretary followed at the India Office and in Foreign Affairs. He was also in great demand as a writer, providing accounts of his travels and political views. In 1898 he became Viceroy to India. After serving as Chancellor of Oxford University he entered Lloyd George's war cabinet, and in 1919, was appointed Foreign Secretary. A Tory reformer and spokesman for Britain's imperial mission, Curzon may be best remembered today for extending knowledge of Indian art, archaeology and literature to the West.

CUSTOM HOUSE QUAY

So named because it faces the Custom House designed by James Gandon. Situated on the riverfront with Beresford Place to the rear, the Custom House is often seen as architecturally the most important building in Dublin. It was the first major public building to be erected in the city as an isolated structure with four monumental façades. The previous Custom House designed by Thomas Burgh was up-river on Essex Quay. It was built in 1707 but only seventy years later was judged unsafe. The site chosen for the new building met with much opposition from city merchants, who feared that the move down-river would lessen the value of their properties while making the property owners to the east wealthier. The decision to build at the new location was forced by the Right Honourable John Beresford (1738–1805), who was Chief Commissioner from 1780 onwards and was instrumental in bringing James Gandon to Ireland. He favoured shifting the city centre eastwards from the Capel Street/Parliament Street area towards a new axis formed by College Green and Drogheda Street (part of present-day O'Connell Street). These two areas were to be linked by the construction of a new bridge across the Liffey at the site of the present O'Connell Bridge, where none had existed prior to this.

The Custom House was constructed on slob land reclaimed from the estuary of the Liffey when the Wide Streets Commissioners developed the quays. The line of the crescent of Beresford Place, which surrounds the Custom House, roughly follows the line of the old North Strand, which ran along the north side of the estuary before the quays were extended. Started in 1781, the new building was completed ten years later at a cost of over £200,000. The external design was made up of four façades, each different yet following a consistent pattern, and linked by corner pavilions. The exterior is richly adorned with sculptures and coats-of-arms designed by Thomas Banks, Agnostino Carlini and Edward

Smyth, who carved a series of sculpted keystones symbolising the rivers of Ireland.

In the Civil War of 1921–2 the building was completely engulfed by a fire following an IRA attack. The fire blazed for five days, destroying a huge quantity of public records. The heat was so intense that the dome melted, and the stonework was still cracking due to cooling five months later. Gandon's interior was completely destroyed. The building underwent major reconstruction, and the dome and drum were completely rebuilt in Ardbraccan limestone (as compared to the original Portland stone). This limestone is of a much darker colour, as can be seen from illustrations. The building was further restored by the Office of Public Works in the 1980s, after it was discovered that the large cornice was in danger of collapsing from the fire damage and rusting of the ironwork braces holding the stonework together. The fine exterior sculptures and coats-of-arms were restored, and a new Portland stone cornice fitted to replace the sub-standard one installed after the fire.

DALYMOUNT

Named after a property developer, Peter Daly, who built this terrace before 1834.

DAME STREET / LANE / COURT

Originally there was a nunnery called Sainte Marie del Dam at the western end of this street, from which all the above derive their names. The convent in turn was named after a dam or mill pond at a nearby crossing of the river Poddle.

A fine street widened in 1769 by the Wide Streets Commissioners, Dame Street has long been the centre of finance in the city, with many fine bank buildings and financial institutions, including the Central Bank of Ireland. This is a very assertive building with a bold outline and dramatic styling, visible throughout the city centre but particularly in Temple Bar, where narrow streets and gaps between buildings reveal its strong geometric presence. The bank was designed by Sam Stephenson and has attracted criticism like several of his other buildings, in this case for its height and original roofline (which contravened the planning permission) as well as for its brash appearance in Temple Bar. Originally the roof was highly distinctive, with its support members outside the roof surface. After problems with rainwater this was redesigned and remodelled using copper cladding to cover the roof structure. It is an unusual building for its time in regard to structure (1970s). The floors are all suspended from the twin service cores at twelve support points by the steel trusses visible on the façades. During construction each floor was built at ground level and then hoisted into place with all its service equipment and fittings in place.

Amongst other buildings of note in Dame Street is the AIB Bank opposite the Olympia Theatre. This was formerly the Munster & Leinster Bank, designed by Thomas Deane in 1872 and based on the design of the museum at Trinity College, almost twenty years older. The bank was built similarly in the Lombardesque-Romanesque idiom, with large round-headed windows and polychromic stone surrounds. The interior banking hall is magnificent, one of the most impressive in Dublin. A vast soaring vaulted ceiling dwarfs customers and bank staff. In 1956 the bank was enlarged, with the main façade sympathetically extended along Dame Street. The extension of the interior, however, was less successful.

Across the street is one of Dublin's main theatres, the Olympia, whose cast-iron and glass canopy straddles the pavement. Plain rendered façades on the street frontage mask a fine Victorian interior.

Dame Court is reached through a narrow passageway from Dame Street. It is chiefly renowned for the *Stag's Head*, one of Dublin's most lavish Victorian gin palaces, which was built in 1895. It is not without reason that Dublin barmen were popularly known as 'curates', and this bar provides a clear example of public house architecture as an almost religious experience. (The architect, A. J. McLaughlin, had previously produced watercolour perspectives of churches.) The exterior has an arcade of round-headed windows down one side, while the main façade has projecting bay windows above the granite and marble of the ground floor. With its panelling, arcading, mirrors and stained glass, the interior is almost as well built and well maintained. Recently immortalised in a Guinness advertising campaign, this bar is well worth a visit.

DANIEL STREET

Named by the Artisans' Dwellings Company in 1887 after the Reverend James Daniel, Parish Priest of St Nicholas of Myra in Francis Street.

DAWSON STREET

Laid out in 1707 and named after Joshua Dawson, who also developed Dawson Street, Grafton Street, South Anne Street and Harry Street, all in this area. Dawson Street is a wide boulevard running straight from St Stephen's Green to Nassau Street, and was once lined with fine houses. Dawson erected a dwelling for himself here in 1710, but never lived in it. It was purchased for £3,500 by the Corporation in 1715 as a residence for the Lord Mayor, and was subsequently extended to form the current Mansion House. The Corporation added external rendering, the fine porch and the adjacent round room, which was built for the visit of George IV and was the venue for the first sitting of Dáil Éireann in 1919.

St Ann's Church is aligned on an axis with Anne Street, and was designed by Thomas Deane in a Lombardo-Romanesque style. The original church on the site was designed by Isaac Wills in 1720, but it was never fully completed and was demolished in 1868 to make way for the current structure. This in turn did not see completion and the northern tower remains without the ornate belfry intended for it, disrupting the flow of the building from the rectory to the spire. (The original tower and spire were to complete the gradual rise in height of the composition.) The interior contains more stained glass than any church in Dublin and includes work by Wilhelmina Geddes, Mayer, Warrington and the O'Connor family. The close proximity of a nearby office block detracts from the impact of many of these windows by reducing the amount of light.

DEAN STREET

Near St Patrick's Cathedral, this was part of the cathedral's Liberty and takes its name from its proximity to the Deanery. Originally it was known as Cross Poddle, and was a crossing point for the now subterranean Poddle river. The Poddle ran alongside Patrick Street but was covered in after a bad flood in 1860.

DEAN SWIFT SQUARE

Named after Jonathan Swift (1667–1745), Dean of nearby St Patrick's Cathedral. Educated at Trinity College, he travelled to England upon graduation to work for Sir William Temple, and later for the Church in the hope of a 'fat deanery or a lean bishopric'. Swift, whose best-known work is the satirical novel *Gulliver's Travels*, was also a successful pamphleteer, and he wrote political pieces for the Tory party while in England. After the Tories' fall from power, he returned to Dublin and took up the position of Dean of St Patrick's. Whilst back in Ireland he wrote a series of anonymous pieces on social issues including 'A Modest Proposal', in which, with heavy satire, he advocated that the poor sell their children for food. After his death he left the bulk of his estate to fund an asylum, St Patrick's Hospital in Steevens' Lane. In his own words:

'He gave the little wealth he had
To build a house for fools and mad
And showed by one satiric touch
No nation wanted it so much.'

The houses in this square are small brick cottages constructed by the Artisans' Dwellings Company.

DENZILLE LANE

Named after Denzille Holles, Earl of Clare, as are nearby Clare Street and Holles Street. Denzille Lane was once home to James Carey, a member of a Fenian splinter group known as the

'Invincibles'. This was the group responsible for the assassinations in the Phoenix Park in 1882 of the Chief Secretary and the Under Secretary, who had been walking near the viceregal lodge. Carey turned informer, resulting in the execution of five associates. He was himself murdered by another member of the Invincibles, Patrick O'Donnell, while en route to South Africa in 1883.

DERRYNANE PARADE
Named after the home of Daniel O'Connell in Co. Kerry, and part of a naming scheme in this area based on beauty spots and other place-names in that county.

DIGGES STREET
Digges Street is probably named after a Huguenot settler named Digges. Nearby Digges Lane was originally called Goat Alley.

DILLON PLACE
Named after the Young Irelander John Blake Dillon (1814–66), who founded *The Nation* newspaper with Charles Gavin Duffy and Thomas Davis.

DOCK STREET SOUTH
So named because of its proximity to the Grand Canal Docks.

D'OLIER STREET
Jeremiah D'Olier (1745–1817), City Sheriff in 1788, was one of the Wide Streets Commissioners. This street was named after him in 1799 when, as Governor of the Bank of Ireland, he proposed to build new headquarters for the bank between College Street and the river, to be designed by Soane. This plan was shelved when the Houses of Parliament became available after the Act of Union in 1801. D'Olier and Westmoreland Streets were the last two major interventions by the Wide Streets Commissioners as part of their plan for Dublin city. The street was built as an integrated and cohesive whole, with four-storey brick façades over stone shop

fronts, probably designed by Aaron Baker. The western side, which now houses the offices of *The Irish Times*, has been restored where possible to its original.

D'Olier Chambers was built in 1891 by J. F. Fuller for Gallagher's Tobacco Company out of yellow brick and terracotta. Cleverly used to turn the corner, the building is prominent with its decorative features, scrolled gables and tall chimneys.

The former headquarters of the Dublin Gas Company, built in 1928, has two façades with different architectural styles. The main façade on D'Olier Street is in the Art Deco style, with strong symmetry and shiny polished stone facing. The shop façade has a stepped low-relief door surround, while the upper lights of the windows all feature etched glass panels. Originally the upper windows had zig-zag motifs in the glazing bars, but these have been removed and more modern frames inserted. The fine interior space still has Art Deco motifs, visible mainly in the columns and ceiling details. The building has been well maintained with the large inset 'Gas' sign still illuminated at night.

O'Connell Bridge House was built in the 1960s and replaced Carlisle House, which was similar in design to the Ballast Office, at the river end of Westmoreland Street. This too has now been demolished and replaced with a facsimile. The rear of the building on Hawkins Street is a strange mix of English Tudor and the style known as Arts and Crafts. While such an eclectic combination of styles should not work, here it is does, perhaps because the two façades do not meet and cannot be seen at the same time.

DOLPHIN'S BARN

First mentioned in 1396, this unusual name in an urban environment probably derives from the name of a family who may have owned land in the area, rather than from the sea mammal.

DOMINICK STREET / LANE / PLACE

Dominick Street was developed by the family of Sir Christopher Dominick in the 1750s and for a time was very fashionable, with some fine houses being developed. It went into terminal decline after the Act of Union and most of the houses had become slums before Dublin Corporation built flats to replace them. Arthur Griffith (1871–1922) lived at No. 4. The stuccodore Robert West, who designed many of the finest interiors in the city, lived at No. 20, a house he designed and decorated himself with very elaborate plasterwork. The writer Joseph Sheridan Le Fanu (1814–73) was born at No. 45, while William Rowan Hamilton (1805–65), the mathematician and inventor of quaternions, was born at No. 36.

St Saviour's Church is perhaps the finest church designed by J. J. McCarthy in Dublin, although it was not completed as originally planned. A proposed tower and spire were never started, the money being used instead to build the adjoining monastery. The church has a fine interior, although it now lacks many of its original features because of the reorganisation that followed the Second Vatican Council. A fine nave with aisles and side chapels leads to a polygonal apse.

DONORE AVENUE

Named after the Liberty of Donore, which was granted to Sir William Brabazon along with the lands of the Friary of St Thomas in the 17th century.

DORSET STREET

This was known as Drumcondra Lane before the Gardiners built up the area. It was renamed in 1756 after Lionel Cranfield Sackville, first Duke of Dorset and Lord Lieutenant in 1731–7 and again in 1751–5. A busy commercial street, it has a fine fire station designed in 1901 by the City Architect, C. J. McCarthy. The writer Seán O'Casey (1880–1964) was born at No. 85 before his family moved to nearby Innisfallen Parade after his father was injured falling off a ladder. No. 12 was the birthplace of Richard Brinsley Sheridan.

DRURY STREET

This was originally known as Little Boater or Butter Lane and was a continuation of Great Boater Street (now Bishop Street). Named Drury Lane around 1766, probably after the Reverend John Drury, it was widened and renamed Drury Street in around 1800 when the South City Markets were constructed.

DUKE STREET / LANE

Developed by Joshua Dawson along with South Anne Street, Dawson Street and Grafton Street, and named after the second Duke of Grafton (1663–90) who had been Viceroy for a time. Duke Street is the location of two of Dublin's more famous literary pubs: the *Bailey* (now bearing little resemblance to its former self) and *Davy Byrne's*. The Bailey was an extremely popular pub and many writers, including Kavanagh, Behan, Gogarty, Pádraic Colum, and Brian O'Nolan drank here. For many years it contained the door of No. 7 Eccles Street, the home of Leopold Bloom in Joyce's *Ulysses*. The Bailey itself is not mentioned in the book, despite being one of Joyce's favourite pubs. Davy Byrne's was frequented by many famous people, including politicians such as Michael Collins and Arthur Griffith, and writers like Behan and Pádraic Ó Conaire. It also features in *Ulysses* as the 'moral pub' where Bloom has his lunch. The adjacent Duke Lane was previously known as Badger's Lane.

EARL STREET NORTH

Developed by Henry Moore, Earl of Drogheda, whose sense of humour and self-worth is reflected in the many streets that bear his name: Henry Street, Moore Street, Earl Street, Of Lane (now disappeared) and Drogheda Street (now O'Connell Street). The Moore estate was purchased in 1714 by Luke Gardiner who developed it further. A statue of James Joyce stands near the junction of Earl Street and O'Connell Street.

EARL STREET SOUTH

This was developed on lands belonging to the Earl of Meath. It was once a street of tenements, eventually demolished. In the early 1990s a development plan involving a high level of civic design was proposed for the street by leading architects involved in the redevelopment of Temple Bar. The plan was never carried out.

EARLSFORT TERRACE

Named after John Scott, Baron Earlsfort, later Earl of Clonmell, after whom Clonmel Street is also named. Most of Earlsfort Terrace has been redeveloped over the years, with large office complexes replacing the former Alexandra Girls' College. Opposite them is the National Concert Hall, built on part of the Coburg Gardens (now Iveagh Gardens), in which the Dublin International Exhibition was held in 1865. The exhibition buildings have seen many changes. First they were converted to be used as examination halls by the Royal University of Ireland; in

1914 they were redeveloped by the architect R. M. Butler in an austere, classical style reflecting that of the Custom House, and finally they were adapted again in the early 1980s to house the National Concert Hall. Parts of the building are still used by UCD, for whom the adaptations by R. M. Butler were made. Until the 1970s, this was a central part of the UCD campus prior to the development of Belfield.

ECCLES STREET / PLACE

Sir John Eccles was Lord Mayor in 1710 and owned some property here. His house, Mount Eccles, stood where the Loreto Convent in North Great George's Street now stands, and he built St George's Church (a chapel of ease) in Lower Temple Street for his Protestant tenants. (This street became Hill Street in 1886.) Until the 1980s, this was a fine intact Georgian street, before the Mater Hospital obtained permission to demolish the north side to build an extension to the hospital. Much of the south side of the street is also in disrepair. The home of Leopold and Molly Bloom in Joyce's *Ulysses* was at No. 7 Eccles Street, which has now been demolished, although the door has been preserved and is on display in the Joyce Centre in North Great George's Street.

The architect Francis Johnston (1760–1829) lived at No. 64 Eccles Street. He came originally from Armagh, and he studied in Dublin with another famous architect, Thomas Cooley. In 1805 Johnston was appointed architect to the Board of Works. Among the principal buildings he designed in Dublin are the GPO (General Post Office) and St George's Church in Hardwicke Place; he was also responsible for converting the former Houses of Parliament on College Green for the use of the Bank of Ireland. He worked in many architectural styles – the Chapel Royal in Dublin Castle is an example of his interpretation of Gothic – while his country houses include the castellated Charleville Forest in Co. Offaly. Johnston also designed the Mock Tudor Gothic gateway to the Royal Hospital Kilmainham. One of the founders of the Royal Hibernian Academy, he was president of that body between 1824 and 1829.

ECHLIN STREET

Named after the Reverend Henry Echlin, who was vicar of St Catherine's in Thomas Street around 1760. He later became vicar of St James's, where he died while vicar in 1752.

EDEN QUAY

Named after a former Chief Secretary to Ireland (1780–92), William Eden, who asked John Beresford to name a street or square after him if their combined plans for Dublin should ever come to fruition. In a letter to Beresford he wrote: 'If our great plans should ever go into execution for the improvement of Dublin, I beg that you will contrive to edge my name into some street or into some square, opening to a bridge, the bank or the four courts.'

Eden Quay is the location of what is certainly not the most popular building in Dublin but is currently the tallest, namely Liberty Hall, the headquarters of the SIPTU trade union. This was built on the site of the earlier Liberty Hall, a rebel mobilising point in the 1916 rising. Started in 1961 and finished in 1965, Liberty Hall has sixteen storeys and is 195 feet tall. The top-floor pavilion commands an excellent view over the entire city from a viewing deck which was open to the public for a brief period around the late 1960s. At the time of its construction, Liberty Hall was fitted with non-reflective glass which gave the building a wonderfully translucent effect. A bomb explosion in 1972 blew out most of the glass, which was replaced with a reflective variety. (The viewing deck was also closed at this time.) The building has lost a lot of its original impact because of this. The top-floor pavilion makes a 'nod' of acknowledgement designwise to the nearby and vastly superior Busáras with its angled cap and mosaic tiles on the underside of the canopy.

ELGIN ROAD

Named after James Bruce (1811–63), eighth Earl of Elgin, who was Governor General of India in the early 1860s. This is one of many fine red-brick terraces in the Ballsbridge area, which the writer Elizabeth Bowen referred to in her autobiography *Seven Winters* as the 'red roads'. Built between 1846 and 1857, many of them had names of military origin.

ELLIS QUAY / STREET

Named after the Agar Ellis family, Viscounts of Clifden, who obtained from the Corporation in the 17th century a valuable leasehold reaching from Arran Quay westwards to the Phoenix Park. Some of the leases are dated 1662 and their maps show the Liffey as the southern boundary of the Ellis property. Ellis Street is shown on Rocque's map of 1756 as Cuffe Street, but by 1780 it was known as Silver Street. It was immortalised under this name in 1890 by Rudyard Kipling in a poem called 'Belts', about a fight involving soldiers from the barracks and the local people. The street was renamed Ellis Street in 1892.

ELY PLACE

Developed by Sir Gustavus Hume MP and so named because the first house here was leased to Henry Loftus, Viscount of Ely (later Earl of Ely) who married Hume's daughter. Originally the upper part of Ely Place was named Smith's Buildings after a builder, Thomas Smith, who lived at No. 1 from 1836 to 1849. This name was not deemed grand enough by the residents, who had it changed to Upper Ely Place. Ely House, facing down Hume Street, was designed by the stuccodore Michael Stapleton, and contains fine ceilings and an impressive staircase. It is now the headquarters of the Knights of Columbanus, and doubled as the Embassy of the United Kingdom in a recent BBC television series. No. 6, which also has a fine Stapleton interior, was the home of the Earl of Clare, John Fitzgibbon, who, although a staunch supporter of the Union and very much against Catholic emancipation, was a friend of Thomas Fitzgerald and was observed to weep at the news of Fitzgerald's death. In the early 1970s some houses were demolished at the upper end of the street to build the Gallagher Gallery for the Royal Hibernian Academy.

EMMET STREET

Named after Robert Emmet (1778–1803), Irish patriot and martyr. As a member of the United Irishmen, he attempted to lead an uprising against Dublin Castle in July 1803, in the hope that a spontaneous popular rebellion would follow across the country. After attempting to win assistance from France, Emmet moved the date of the uprising forward, but only a small minority of the expected insurgents gathered in Dublin. When the attack on the Castle failed, the force took control for a few hours of the area around James's Street and Thomas Street, before being dispersed by soldiers. About fifty people were killed, including a former Attorney General and the Lord Chief Justice. Emmet was arrested in the Wicklow mountains. His defence speech in court became widely read as a classic of Irish nationalist literature. He was executed on 20 September 1803 outside St Catherine's Church in Thomas Street.

EMPRESS PLACE

Named after Queen Victoria, Empress of India.

ENGINE ALLEY

In Rocque's map of 1756 this is marked as Indian Alley, of which the present name is probably a corruption.

ERNE STREET

Near Creighton Street, it is named after the Creighton family, Earls of Erne. The Creightons married into the family of Rogerson, who developed this area in the early 18th century.

ESSEX GATE / QUAY / STREET

The short section of street between Parliament Street and Exchange Street, which was once the site of a gate to the medieval city, is today called Essex Gate. It is named after the Earl of Essex, a member of the Capel family, who was Viceroy for a period. The gate was removed early in the 18th century.

Essex Street was previously known as Orange Street and before that as Smock Alley. Now part of the Temple Bar area, it is the location of the Project Theatre, a new building completed in 2000 by Shay Cleary Architects on the site of a former print works which had been converted for use as a theatre in the 1970s. Other buildings worthy of note include the former Nugent's (now Bob's)– a fine red-brick pub whose interior has unfortunately been removed – and the Dolphin Hotel (now offices), both in the Gothic Revival style. Designed by J. J. O'Callaghan in 1898, the Dolphin Hotel was once home to one of Dublin's most famous restaurants and an early Art Deco cocktail bar. These were all destroyed, but the fine exterior, with its carved dolphins over the diagonal corner entrance, was reprieved.

EUSTACE BRIDGE

Crosses the Grand Canal at Leeson Street. It is named after Colonel Charles Eustace, MP, who was deputy chairman of the canal company in 1791.

EUSTACE STREET

This is named after Sir Maurice Eustace, Speaker of the House of Commons in 1639 and Lord Chancellor in 1644, whose mansion and gardens once stood here. He was responsible together with the Duke of Ormonde for the creation of the Phoenix Park. The Quakers (Society of Friends) opened a meeting house in Eustace Street in 1692; part of the premises is now home to the Irish Film Centre. Designed by O'Donnell and Tuomey, the Film Centre has no discernible street presence, as it was sited at the centre of a pre-existing city block. It does however have three narrow entrance routes – one through a long corridor from Eustace Street, another via a side passage from Dame Street known as Coghill's Court, and a third that passes through a small raised courtyard to the rear, linking it with Meetinghouse Square and Sycamore Street. The main cinema is sited inside the old Quaker meeting room and still has all its original features other than at balcony level. Cinema 2 is upstairs and retains the old roof timbers.

Halfway down Eustace Street is a small entrance and alley-way leading to Meetinghouse Square.

EXCHANGE STREET
Previously known as Scarlet Alley and Isolde's Lane, it acquired its present name for its proximity to the original Royal Exchange. Exchange Street Lower was once known as the Blind Quay and contained warehouses and stores for the former Custom House on Essex Quay. Part of the Temple Bar area, Exchange Street has now been redeveloped with apartments and housing. The former church of St Michael and St John is now used as the Viking Interpretive Centre. Designed by J. Taylor and built in 1815, the church once had a fine interior and ceiling.

EXCHEQUER STREET
The Royal Exchequer was based here in the medieval period, having been established in the late 12th century. Later it was moved to the cloisters of Christ Church Cathedral to protect it from attack by the native Irish. In 1728 the street was known as Chequer Street. Originally it ran as far as Grafton Street, but in 1837 the residents at the Grafton Street end petitioned the Wide Streets Commissioners to have the name changed to Wicklow Street as it was difficult to obtain respectable tenants for the properties.

FADE STREET

Named after Joseph Fade, a banker. A lane known as Joseph Lane ran nearby through what is now the South City Markets, which were built in 1880 and resulted in the widening of Fade Street.

FATHER MATHEW BRIDGE

This bridge, linking Bridge Street and Church Street, is built on the site of what until 1674 was the only bridge across the Liffey. It is named after Fr Theobald Mathew (1790–1856) from Tipperary, a member of the Capuchin order who proposed total abstinence from alcohol and took up the teetotal cause in 1838 with phenomenal success. It is reckoned that by 1842, out of a total population of just over eight million, some five million had taken the teetotal pledge.

There are many records of previous bridges on this site. The Normans built one in 1210, and in 1214 King John gave the city permission to build a new one, which collapsed in 1385. The monks from the nearby Dominican friary replaced this in 1428. Over the years, the bridges have gone by many names: Droichet Dubhgaill; Danes Bridge; Ostmans Bridge; Black Danes Bridge; King John's Bridge; Dublin Bridge; Great Bridge; Old Bridge; and Friars Bridge. The current bridge opened in 1818 and was originally Whitworth Bridge after the Lord Lieutenant of the time, Charles, Earl of Whitworth.

FENIAN STREET

Named after the Fenian Brotherhood (also known as the Irish Republican Brotherhood), a secret organisation simultaneously founded in New York and Dublin on 17 March 1858 and dedicated to the foundation of a democratic Irish republic. The street was formerly known as Denzil or Denzille Street after Denzille Holles, Earl of Clare.

FINDLATER STREET

Named by the Artisans' Dwellings Company after one of its directors, William Findlater, wine merchant and grocer. 'Findlater's' – the family's food and wine stores – was for many years an institution in Dublin.

FINGAL STREET

Probably named after the Earls of Fingal.

FISHAMBLE STREET

This was the site of the fish market in the medieval city: the name is derived from 'fish shambles'. In 1467, it was called Vicus Piscariorium (or fishmongers' quarters). The street ran from Castle Street to Essex Quay until Lord Edward Street was opened in 1886, resulting in the removal of five houses. In the 18th century this was quite a fashionable area. It was the birthplace of Archbishop Ussher, the poet James Clarence Mangan and the politician Henry Grattan. Fishamble Street's main claim to fame however is as the site of the first performance of Handel's *Messiah*, which took place in Mr Neale's Music Hall on 13 April 1742. The event was held in aid of Mercer's Hospital, the Charitable Infirmary and prison relief. A huge crowd attended, and legend has it that in order to create more space, men were asked to come without swords and ladies without hoops in their skirts. On 28 February 1812, the great orator and Irish statesman Daniel O'Connell addressed a packed theatre in the same venue. The

Music Hall was built in 1741 to the design of Richard Cassels and was in use until the 19th century. It is now gone, but a facsimile of the entrance archway has recently been erected on the same site after the original collapsed.

FITZGIBBON STREET

Named after John Fitzgibbon (1749–1802), Lord Chancellor from 1789 to 1802 and created Earl of Clare in 1795. Fitzgibbon was a determined opponent of Irish nationalism and Catholic emancipation. The son of a wealthy lawyer who was a convert from Catholicism, he was strongly in favour of the Act of Union of 1801 and a leading advocate of the tough security measures taken after the 1798 rebellion. Although he was an 'improving' landlord, there were violent demonstrations at his funeral.

FITZWILLIAM STREET

Named after the Fitzwilliam family, Earls of Merrion, who developed the area as part of their great estate which was laid out on the south side of the Liffey between 1750 and 1850. Their first project was Merrion Street in 1758. The land acquired by the Fitzwilliams was leased from the City Corporation in a single parcel, making theirs the most cohesive estate in Dublin, unlike that of the Gardiner family which was bought and developed in small parcels. Dublin's Georgian houses are characterised by the façade design found in this area, particularly in Fitzwilliam Street, Fitzwilliam Square, Mount Street Upper and Merrion Square. The visual integrity and uniformity of the Georgian exteriors masks the wealth of variety adorning the interiors, many of which have magnificent plasterwork ceilings and ornate fireplaces and staircases.

The longest expanse of intact Georgian architecture in the world was destroyed in 1965 when a semi-state body, the Electricity Supply Board, demolished sixteen houses in Fitzwilliam Street.

Until then, this had presented an unbroken line of almost a mile of Georgian houses passing through Fitzwilliam Square and Merrion Square. The ESB removed most of the left-hand side of Lower Fitzwilliam Street between the two squares in order to develop new headquarters – a poor example of modern architecture designed by Sam Stephenson.

FITZWILLIAM SQUARE

Fitzwilliam Square is still very much a residential square with the park in the centre reserved for the use of residents and property owners. The square was started in 1791 but was not completed until the early part of the 19th century. Famous past residents have included the artists Mainie Jellet (No. 36) and Jack B. Yeats (No. 18); and William Dargan, the railway engineer and public works contractor (No. 2).

FITZWILLIAM QUAY

A quay on the Dodder River near the Grand Canal Docks where it enters the Liffey. It is named for the Fitzwilliam family, probably after Richard, the seventh Viscount, who died in 1816.

FLEET STREET

Originally this marked the edge of the south bank of the Liffey, which continued along Temple Bar. The name probably derives from the Anglo-Saxon word 'fleet', meaning a tidal inlet. The ferry which operated from the end of Fleet Alley may have used such an inlet in the riverbank as a mooring place. (Fleet Alley disappeared with the construction of Westmoreland Street.) The republican Kevin Barry (1902–20), the subject of many ballads, was born at No. 8. Captured while taking part in a raid in Church Street, he was the first member of the IRA to be executed in the War of Independence.

The Palace Bar, one of Dublin's finest pubs, has a strong literary tradition that is partly attributable to its proximity to the offices of

The Irish Times. From five o'clock every evening the paper's legendary editor from the 1930s onwards, Robert M. Smyllie, held court here with the likes of Brinsley MacNamara, Austin Clark, Patrick Kavanagh and the English poet John Betjeman, who was based at the British Embassy during the Emergency.

FOLEY STREET

Once known as World's End Lane because its eastern end, where it joined what was then known as the Strand and where the shore began, was called World's End. It was later named Montgomery Street after Elizabeth Montgomery, who married Luke Gardiner, an important property owner in the area. The street gave its name to Dublin's notorious red-light district, the 'Monto', which also included nearby Railway Street (previously Mecklenburgh Street), and which features in the 'Nighttown' episode in Joyce's *Ulysses*. It was once the largest such area in Europe, recorded as having over 1,600 prostitutes in the period 1800–1900. The Monto continued to operate successfully even after the departure of the British troops in 1922, but a Lenten raid by gardai and Catholic vigilantes in 1925 resulted in 120 arrests and delivered a deathblow to the area. In the 1930s all the original terraces were demolished and replaced by Corporation flats.

FONTENOY STREET

Laid out between 1872 and 1880 and named after a battle in present-day Belgium in 1745 in which the French defeated the English with the assistance of an Irish brigade.

FORBES STREET

Named after a land agent named Forbes who was responsible for disposal of the South Lotts.

FOSTER PLACE

Known as Turnstile Alley before it was widened and renamed after

John Foster (1740–1828), last Speaker of the House of Commons in the Irish Parliament, who was also one of the Wide Streets Commissioners. This is a cul-de-sac leading to the former Central Bank building, dominated by the curving screen wall and portico of the former Houses of Parliament. Cobbled and tree-lined, it is a popular street for filming as it requires little work to set the scene for period drama here.

Worthy of note but frequently overlooked is the building housing a branch of Allied Irish Banks. This was previously the head office of the Royal Bank of Ireland, which merged with the Provincial Bank and Munster & Leinster Bank to form AIB in 1966. The exterior is a fairly straightforward example of classicism, with a neo-classical porch added in 1850. It is the interior however that makes this building important. It contains the finest banking hall in Dublin, added to the rear of the building by Charles Geoghegan in 1859. This has a coffered barrel-vaulted ceiling, top-lit and supported by cast-iron Corinthian columns. The unusually high entrance hall creates a barrier between the banking hall and the street. An arcaded mezzanine for supervising the counter staff was planned but never built. The counter itself is over 120 feet long with opulent carving and curves.

FOWNES STREET

Named after Sir William Fownes, Lord Mayor of Dublin in 1708–09, who had a medieval mansion in this area, with gardens stretching down to the riverside. The lower part of the street was known as the Bagnio Slip – from 'bagnio', meaning brothel – after a local establishment. The buildings on the right hand side from Dame Street to Cope Street were demolished to make way for the new Central Bank and plaza, which was opened in 1978. The clearance of the site for this purpose also meant that Fownes Court, where the home of William Fownes had once stood, was swept away. Fownes Court had also contained the first maternity hospital in the United Kingdom or Ireland (1742) which was later moved and called The Rotunda after its new accommodation, the General Post Office (1783), various schools and a charitable infirmary. It was eventually taken over by a group of merchants and traders, and a complex known as the Commercial Buildings, designed by Edward Parke, was erected here in 1796. All of these buildings were removed in the 1970s. The stones of the old Commercial Buildings were numbered, as later re-assembly was planned on the site. In the end, however, the Central Bank opted instead to build a facsimile of the old building with new materials. It is situated on a corner of the site.

FRANCIS STREET

Originally known as St Francis Street for its proximity to the mendicant friary of St Francis founded by Ralph de Porter in 1235. The grounds were granted to William Hande after the dissolution of the monasteries in 1537. Now best known for its abundance of antique shops, Francis Street has two fine buildings of note: the former Iveagh Markets dating from 1902, and St Nicholas of Myra, one of Dublin's finest neo-classical churches. The market building (now closed) is a solid construction of red brick with stone dressings with a cast-iron galleried market-hall. The church was built by John Leeson between 1829 and 1834. Later work was carried out in 1858 by Patrick Byrne, who closed off some of the windows to create a better setting for works of sculpture. With a richly ornate interior, the church is the only one in the city to still have its original altar rails – after the Second Vatican Council these were generally removed.

FRANK SHERWIN BRIDGE

Built in 1982 as part of an effort to reorganise traffic flows along the quays and relieve congestion at Sarah Bridge. It was named for a populist city councillor and TD.

FREDERICK STREET NORTH

Possibly named after Frederick the Great of Prussia (1712–86), but it is more likely that the name comes from Dr Frederick Jebb, Master of the Rotunda Hospital in 1773, whose father was responsible for developing the street. Frederick Jebb was also a regular contributor of political essays to *The Freeman's Journal* under the name 'Guatimozin'. The artist in stained glass Harry Clarke (1889–1931) had his renowned studios at Nos. 6–7.

FREDERICK STREET SOUTH

Originally known as Library Street because it faced the former Library of Trinity College, designed by Thomas Burgh. It was later named after Frederick (1707–51), eldest son of George II, who is the only member of the British royal family ever to die from the blow of a cricket ball. The street has some fine houses dating from the 1750s, although many others have been demolished to make way for office developments.

FRIARY AVENUE

Part of a network of ancient narrow streets in the Smithfield area and probably named for its proximity to the Capuchin friary at Church Street, or perhaps the older but now disappeared Dominican friary of St Saviour's, which stood in the vicinity of the present Four Courts.

FUMBALLY LANE

A lease of 1741 refers to a Fombily Lane, and to two houses leased to skinners David and Anthony Fombily.

SRÁID GARDINER
GARDINER STREET

GARDINER STREET / ROW / PLACE

Named after the second Luke Gardiner (1745–98), who laid out much of the Gardiner estate in this part of Dublin. At one time the Gardiners owned twenty-five percent of the city between the canals. The first Luke Gardiner was responsible for developing Henrietta Street, and later for creating Sackville Mall on what had previously been Drogheda Street, having purchased the land from the Moores. This now forms part of O'Connell Street. The second Luke Gardiner opened up new streets on the Eccles Estate; developed Gardiner Street; and laid out Mountjoy Square (1792–1818). He was killed leading the Dublin Militia at the Battle of New Ross in 1798.

In Rocque's map of 1756, Gardiner Street was shown as Old Rope Walk. It was developed as a series of sloping terraces leading from the crescent of Beresford Place on a radius from the Custom House to the proposed new square almost three-quarters of a mile away. This is shown on one of the proposed designs for Mountjoy Square with a note: 'Gardiner's Street extending in a right line from the centre of the new Custom House'. Until the completion of the railway bridge at the southern end of the street, the Custom House provided a magnificent ending for the vista.

Extending from Rutland Square (now Parnell Square) to Temple Street, Gardiner's Row was laid out in 1768 to unite two areas developed by the Gardiner estate. The eastern part was renamed

Great Denmark Street in 1792 when the street was extended to Mountjoy Square.

GEORGE'S QUAY
Probably named after George I, although Brooking's map of 1728 refers to it as St George's Quay.

GLENGARRIFF PARADE
Off the North Circular Road, this was named to a pattern in the area of street-names recalling places in Co. Kerry.

GLOUCESTER STREET SOUTH/ GLOUCESTER PLACE / TERRACE
Named after William Henry, Duke of Gloucester. Nearby Seán MacDermott Street was previously known as Gloucester Street North.

GLOVER'S ALLEY
Just off St Stephen's Green and known as Rapparee Alley until 1766. Rapparee was an Irish term for a robber or bandit. The lane seems to have been renamed for the many glove-makers working in the area.

GOLDEN LANE
From the goldsmiths' guild hall formerly located here. It was called Crosse Lane in records from 1466 and up until the early 1600s.

GOLDSMITH STREET
Named after Oliver Goldsmith (1728–74), the poet, novelist and playwright from Co. Longford. He was educated at Trinity College where he was admitted as a 'sizar' with reduced fees in return for work around the college. After graduation Goldsmith returned home to Longford for a time while awaiting his planned entrance to holy orders. Refused by the Church he started

travelling, first to Edinburgh where he studied medicine but took no degree and then to the continent, finally arriving in London in 1756, destitute at the age of twenty-eight. Failing to get a medical post in India, he started writing, first for *Griffith's Monthly* and later as a poet, novelist and playwright. This brought him great success, but he remained unable to manage his finances and died owing £2,000. A memorial to him was erected in Poet's Corner in Westminster Abbey. His statue was erected outside Trinity College in 1864 near that of his friend Edmund Burke.

GRAFTON STREET

Named after the first Duke of Grafton (1663–90), illegitimate son of Charles II, who owned land in this area. The street was developed by the Dawson family in 1708 from an existing country lane. The opening of the new Carlisle Bridge across the Liffey (where O'Connell Bridge now stands) in 1798 transformed Grafton Street from a fashionable residential street into a busy cross-city route. It is now the main commercial street on the south side of the city, pedestrianised and popular with street entertainers. At the junction with Suffolk Street stands a statue to Dublin's best-known fishmonger, Molly Malone.

Hidden behind high walls at No. 1 is the house of the Provost of Trinity College, said to be the only residential address left in Grafton Street. A sumptuous dwelling, the Provost's House was built by Provost Andrews when he was elected to the post in the 1760s, and it is an accurate reflection of his taste, for it remains as it was when completed. Andrews was a remarkable man, a Member of the House of Commons, a Fellow of Trinity at twenty-one and a Doctor of Law at twenty-six. At that time the position of Provost was held until death, the next incumbent being elected by the Fellows of the college. Many of those who held it assumed prominence in the affairs of the city beyond the college walls.

Externally the house resembles one built by Lord Burlington in

London in the 1730s. It is of solid Palladian design with a central Venetian window and Doric pilasters. It is the interior however that makes it one of the most important buildings in Dublin and one of the most elaborately decorated houses of the period. The dominant room is the saloon which takes up the entire first floor to the front. Although columns at either end visually shorten it, this is still an enormous room, with its coffered ceiling and five windows. The plasterwork is by Patrick and John Wall.

GRANBY ROW
Named after John Manners, Marquess of Granby, a cavalry commander in the Seven Years' War and one of the most famous soldiers of his day. Nearby Rutland Square (now Parnell Square) later (in 1791) took its name from his son, Charles Manners, fourth Duke of Rutland, who was Viceroy for three years and died while still in office as Lord Lieutenant in 1787. John Manners did not live long enough to succeed to the dukedom.

GRAND CANAL QUAY / PLACE / STREET
In 1755 work started on the Grand Canal to link Dublin with the rivers Shannon and Barrow. When it opened to cargo traffic in 1779, it ended near the City Basin off James's Street, but by 1791 it had reached Ringsend, where the Grand Canal Docks opened in 1796. The two basins here together encompass an area of over twenty-five acres. Hanover Quay and Charlotte Quay bound the larger basin, north and south; Grand Canal Quay runs along the west side of both basins, some fine stone warehouses separating it from the quayside. The Docks were officially opened by the Earl of Camden and one of the large locks that separate the basins from the Liffey was named after him. The other two are the Buckingham Lock and the Westmoreland Lock.

GRAND CANAL STREET was known as Artichoke Road until 1792, when its name was changed following the opening of the canal. John Villiboise leased land and erected a house here in 1736, growing artichokes in the garden. The local inhabitants came to know it as 'the artichoke' and eventually this name came to be applied to the street also. A terrace of houses built on the street in 1836 was named Wentworth Terrace after Thomas Wentworth, Earl of Stafford.

GRAND PARADE

A continuation of Mespil Road, Grand Parade runs along a tree-lined stretch of the Grand Canal, from which it derives its name. Once a fashionable place to live, it is now mainly offices. One of the most important mid-20th century buildings in Ireland is located here. Designed and built in 1962–4 by the firm of Robinson Keefe Devane as offices for Carroll's Tobacco Group, this is now the headquarters of the Irish Nationwide Building Society. The building consists of office space on pilotis or columns over a recessed mezzanine level and open ground floor. Both the mezzanine level and the ground floor – three-quarters of which is open, with small pools and bench seating accessible to the public – were used as public spaces and made available for lectures and art exhibitions. The original lecture hall is now used as a banking hall. At the time of its construction the building was noted for its well-lit office space, with floor-to-ceiling windows front and rear and interesting staircases visible through the gable stairwell.

GRANGEGORMAN

The priory of Holy Trinity once owned the manor of Glasnevin and Gorman, and this is reflected in the name Grange (of) Gorman. The lands and buildings belong to various medical and religious institutions dominate Grangegorman.

GRATTAN BRIDGE / STREET

Named after Sir Henry Grattan (1745–1820), a prominent number of the Irish Commons in the Houses of Parliament in

College Green. Indeed the Commons was to become known as 'Grattan's Parliament'. The son of a Dublin lawyer, Grattan first entered Parliament in 1775 and remained there until 1787 when he withdrew due to his disaffection with the government's reactionary response to public disaffection. He returned to Parliament in 1799 to oppose the Act of Union. In 1804 he entered Westminster as an MP to support Catholic Emancipation. A statue commemorates him in College Green.

GRATTAN BRIDGE was formerly known as Essex Bridge after Arthur Capel, Earl of Essex, before being renamed in 1875. The original bridge on the site was built in 1678. It was replaced by another, which collapsed in 1751. Later, in 1722, a statue of George I on horseback was erected on the bridge, but this was removed during further rebuilding in 1753. George Semple was employed to design and build the replacement bridge, which lasted until 1872, when it was decided to eliminate the gradient. A new bridge was constructed on the existing piers, with a carriageway equal in width to the full width of the previous bridge. The new pavements were cantilevered out from the bridge on wrought ironwork. Fine ornamental lamp standards decorated with sea horses are mounted on the metal parapets.

GRAY STREET

Named after Edmund Dwyer Gray, MP (1845–88) by the Artisans' Dwellings Company. It is a fine street of small brick dwellings, with an unusual cast-iron centrepiece built as a water fountain in 1898. This now houses a statue of Christ, erected in 1929 to mark a centenary of Catholic emancipation.

GREAT DENMARK STREET

Part of Gardiner's Row until 1792 when it was renamed after Prince George of Denmark, husband of Queen Anne. As Lord High Admiral, Prince George facilitated the establishment of a

Ballast Office in Dublin. Michael Stapleton (1770–1803), considered to be the most important stuccodore of the Georgian period in Ireland, lived here. Among his most important interiors in Dublin were the Powerscourt Townhouse; the chapel at Trinity College; and Belvedere House, of which he was also the architect. Belvedere House has been occupied by the Jesuits since 1841. His own house, which stood next to it, was demolished in 1968.

GREAT WESTERN SQUARE / AVENUE / VILLAS
This area was developed to provide housing for workers at the nearby Broadstone Station, the Dublin terminus of the Midland and Great Western Railway Company.

GREEK STREET
Formerly known as Cow Lane and Fisher's Lane. Nearby Latin Street suggests that a naming pattern exists.

GREEN STREET / GREEN STREET LITTLE
Green Street was known as Abbey Green in 1558 – the Green of St Mary's Abbey – while Little Green Street was simply Little Green, having originally been called Bradogue Lane after the river that entered the Liffey at nearby Ormond Quay. The smaller street appears on Rocque's map of 1756 as Petticoat Lane. Green Street is the location of the Special Criminal Court, and Newgate Prison once stood here also, on a site that is now a public park. The courthouse designed by Whitmore Davis, which also has a façade on Halston Street, was the scene of many trials including those of Wolfe Tone, Robert Emmet and other Fenian leaders. Lord Edward Fitzgerald died here from injuries incurred during his arrest by Major Sirr.

GREENVILLE AVENUE
Originally named Roper's Rest after Thomas Roper, Viscount Baltinglass.

GRENVILLE STREET

Named after George Grenville Nugent Temple, third Earl Temple and later Marquis of Buckingham, who was Lord Lieutenant in 1782–3 and 1787–9. Surrounding streets such as Temple Street and Buckingham Street also bear his name.

GUILD STREET

Part of the North Lotts, this street is named after the old city guilds from which the Corporation was traditionally formed. There were twenty-five Dublin guilds in all, each holding a given number of seats on the Corporation. This method of electing that body existed until 1840. The only surviving guild is known as the Company of Goldsmiths (or the Guild of All Saints), which continues to assay and hallmark goods made of precious metals. Some of the streets surrounding Guild Street are named after important civic functions, e.g. Mayor Street and Sheriff Street.

HADDINGTON PLACE / ROAD

Named after the Earl of Haddington, Lord Lieutenant in 1834–5 Haddington Road was previously called Cottage Terrace. Part of the Pembroke estates, this became a fashionable residential area in the 19th century.

HALPIN'S ROW

Named after George Halpin, Inspector of Works to the Ballast Board. This was the body with responsibility for the Liffey, its bridges, the port and the lighthouses of Dublin. Halpin was an unusual engineer who held the post for fifty-four years despite his lack of academic qualifications or formal training. He died while on duty. Among his many achievements were the creation of the quay walls downstream of O'Connell Bridge and the replacement of the parapet wall at Inns Quay with a balustrade instead of solid masonry. He was also responsible for overseeing the construction of Fr Mathew Bridge and O'Donovan Rossa Bridge, and was significantly involved in the construction of the Bull Wall and upgrading of the South Wall.

HALSTON STREET

The name derives from Halfstone Street. This was the location of the former Newgate prison, now a public park. Green Street courthouse faces onto it. In 1891 George Ashlin rebuilt St Michan's Church (originally built on Anne Street North) with a new façade and a tower facing onto Halston Street.

HAMILTON STREET

Named after Andrew Hamilton, sexton of nearby St Catherine's Church, who built houses here.

HAMMOND LANE

Hammond Lane was once known as Hangman Lane, which later became Hamon Lane, from which Hammond Lane derives.

HANOVER QUAY / LANE / STREET

Named after George I of Hanover. Hanover Quay faces onto the Grand Canal Docks rather than the Liffey and has low brick warehouses set back from the water's edge.

HARBOURMASTER PLACE

Located within the complex of buildings that today make up the International Financial Services Centre at the heart of the rejuvenated Dublin docklands. The office of the Harbourmaster was once situated here between two docks. It is now a bar and restaurant.

HARCOURT STREET

A largely intact fine Georgian street leading off St Stephen's Green and named after Lord Simon Harcourt, Lord Lieutenant of Ireland from 1772 to 1776. The underground river Stein runs beneath the upper end of the street; a large office development on the corner of Harcourt Street and Hatch Street is named after it. No. 4 was the birthplace of Edward Carson (1854–1935), the father of Ulster Unionism, who represented Trinity College as a Unionist MP at Westminster. An apartment at No. 16 was for a time the home of Bram Stoker (1847–1912), creator of *Dracula*.

The most impressive building in the street is the former Harcourt Street Station, the railway terminus which remained in continuous use from its construction in 1859 until 1959. It is a monumental building on a plinth of steps with a central arch flanked by two colonnades. The design is characterised by simple large-scale details such as the corbels supporting the central portico above the paired columns. The original platforms were at first floor level as the railway line was built on an embankment. On one occasion the train from Bray failed to stop and the locomotive plunged through the end wall of the building, providing one of the most enduring photographic images of the station.

Beneath the station shed are the arched vaults originally designed to be a bonded spirit store; they now house Findlater's wine merchant's premises and one of Dublin's most fashionable night-spots. The main part of the building to the front has recently been renovated, cleaned and turned into a bar that gives an impression of enormous size not suggested by the station's external dimensions. The design of the bar is sympathetic to the original and manages to suggest a Victorian gentlemen's club without descending into pastiche.

HARCOURT TERRACE
Prior to the building of the Garda Station on its eastern side, this short street close to Harcourt Street was enclosed by railings and gated. It includes a fine terrace of houses with neo-classical style façades added to the existing Georgian houses around 1840. Some of the houses have been restored. Only the façade of the centrepiece at Nos. 6 and 7 is original, the houses having been converted to modern office accommodation. The actor and director Hilton Edwards lived at No. 4 with Mícheál MacLiammóir, actor and playwright (1899–1978). Best known as the founders of the Gate Theatre in 1928, they formed the most celebrated partnership in the history of Irish theatre, producing most of the plays at the Gate for almost fifty years.

HARDWICKE STREET / PLACE
Developed with St George's Church in the centre and named after

the third Earl of Hardwicke, Lord Lieutenant from 1801 to 1806. This was originally intended to be part of a large urban set-piece with a Royal Circus designed by Francis Johnston at the other end of Eccles Street. The plan was never fulfilled, and the grand Georgian houses that once framed St George's have now been replaced by Corporation flats. The church, designed by Johnston and begun in 1802, is considered architecturally to be one of the finest buildings in Dublin. The 180-foot spire modelled by Johnston on that of St Martin's-in-the-Fields in London is a landmark across the city.

HAROLD ROAD

One of several streets named according to a pattern reflecting the Viking and ancient Irish origins of the area once known as Ostmanstown, now Oxmanstown.

HARRINGTON STREET

This is a pleasant tree-lined street of large brick houses off busy Camden Street. It is named after a former Lord Mayor of Dublin. Harrington Street Church, designed by Pugin and Ashlin, was built between 1867 and 1872. With neither tower nor spire and with a very shallow apse, this unusual Gothic building looks curiously stunted.

HARRY STREET

Named after Harry Dawson, a member of the Dawson family, who developed this area around Grafton Street. In the 18th century, Balfe Street (around the corner at the Westbury Hotel) part of this street. Harry Street contains two famous pubs. Originally the city morgue, McDaid's was also a church for a time before becoming one of Dublin's best-known literary pubs, the haunt of writers such as Patrick Kavanagh, Brian O'Nolan (better known as Flann O'Brien or Myles na gCopaleen) and Brendan Behan. The central character of J. P. Donleavy's novel, *The Ginger Man*, was based on another regular customer, Gainor Christ. Across the street, *The Bruxelles* (formerly Mooney's) is an elaborate brick and stone pub in the Flemish Gothic style, with a corbelled staircase turret overhanging the street. Designed by J. J. O'Callaghan, the interiors are lavishly decorated with painting and mosaics.

HARTY PLACE
Named by the Artisans' Dwellings Company after Spencer Harty.

HATCH STREET / LANE
The Leeson family owned this area, and in 1759 they let sites to John Hatch, after whom the street is named. A director of the Royal Canal Company, Hatch was also a lawyer and lived nearby in Harcourt Street. The street was completely residential when built, but it now consists mainly of offices. The exception is University Hall, built in 1913 as a student residence run by the Jesuits. This is probably the strangest 20th century building in Dublin, and definitely represents 'the last hurrah' for Victorian Gothic in buildings owned by religious institutions. It was designed by C. B. Powell, a Dublin eccentric known as 'God-on-a-bike' because of his long wide beard and mode of travel. Erected around a quadrangle, the building is very well detailed, with stained glass by Evie Hone and a fine oriel window that appears to rest on a slender column.

HAWKINS STREET
In 1662 Alderman William Hawkins built a wall from Townsend Street to Burgh Quay to contain the river. He was granted the land and constructed a street which was originally named Hawkins Quay, until more land was reclaimed from the Liffey. William Mercer was given permission by the City Corporation to fill in this area in the early 1770s, thus forming the quayside known as Mercer Dock. This later became George's Quay after further infill. The line of Mercer Dock is now the northern edge of Poolbeg

Street. Hawkins Street was the location for over a hundred years of the famous Theatre Royal. The last building to be occupied by the theatre was demolished in 1962, to be replaced by a large office block and cinema.

HAYMARKET
A wide expanse of ground linking Queen Street to the larger market space of Smithfield, this was the site of the hay market in medieval times.

HENDRICK STREET / PLACE
Named after Robert Hendrick, City Sheriff in 1707.

HENRIETTA STREET / LANE / PLACE
Henrietta Street dates from the 1720s and was laid out by Luke Gardiner as his first venture in urban development. Gardiner, more than anyone else, was responsible for turning Dublin into an elegant Georgian city. Named after Henrietta, Duchess of Grafton, this street is a cul-de-sac terminating at the archway of the King's Inns, which was designed as an enclave of prestigious houses. The street is still cobbled but many of the fine houses are now in disrepair. In the mid 1700s it was inhabited by five peers, a peeress, a peer's son, a judge, an MP, a bishop and two wealthy clergymen, as well as by Luke Gardiner himself. Edward Lovett Pearce, who also designed the Houses of Parliament on College Green, designed Nos. 9 and 10. At the top end of the street next to the King's Inns is the Law Library designed in 1827 by Frederick Darley. This replaced three of the oldest houses on the street. The interior of No. 9 Henrietta Street has an excellent staircase and hall which can be seen (afternoons, April to September) through the courtesy of the Sisters of Charity. Henrietta Place was shown in Rocque's map of 1756 as Stable Lane, a name given to many back laneways and narrow streets.

HENRY STREET

Developed by Henry Moore, Earl of Drogheda, whose estate and the urban developments he undertook are reflected in the streets in this area that bear his name: Henry Street, Moore Street, Earl Street, Of Lane and Drogheda Street. Moore purchased this land in 1614 from James Fitzgerald, Earl of Desmond, to whom it had been granted when St Mary's Abbey was dismantled. It was later sold to Luke Gardiner, in the early 18th century. Henry Street is a busy pedestrianised shopping street with some fine 19th century commercial buildings, the best of which is Arnott's department store. Designed by G. P. Butler in 1894, this brick building once had an elaborate clock tower, unfortunately removed in 1949. Between Henry Street and Princes Street North is the GPO Arcade, a wide arcaded passageway.

HERBERT STREET / PARK / PLACE

Named after the Right Honourable Sidney Herbert (1810–61), owner of the Fitzwilliam estate after the death of the seventh Viscount Fitzwilliam of Merrion. The composer Charles Villiers Stanford (1852–1924) was born at No. 2 Herbert Street. Herbert Place is a quiet street of elegant Georgian houses running alongside the Grand Canal from Lower Baggot Street to Warrington Place. The writer Elizabeth Bowen (1899–1973) was born at No. 15 and lived here until she was seven.

HEYTESBURY STREET

Named after the first Earl of Heytesbury, Lord Lieutenant from 1844 to 1846. Originally it was intended that this street should go all the way from Portobello Harbour on the Grand Canal to New Bride Street.

HIGH STREET

The principal street of medieval Dublin and possibly called High Street because of its position along a ridge overlooking the river

Liffey. It was decimated by street widening and redevelopment in the 1970s and 1980s, and few of its original buildings remain. Among them is St Audoen's, one of the oldest churches in Dublin, built in 1190 to replace an earlier structure dedicated to St Colmcille. Three bells dating from 1423, said to be the oldest church bells in Ireland, hang in the tower. An early Christian gravestone known as the Lucky Stone is stored in the porch. It has been here since before 1309 and many strange legends are associated with it. Some of the church lies in ruins, and only the main nave is used for services. The Office of Public Works recently restored and re-roofed St Ann's Guild Chapel, the blocked-off south transept of the church, which had been without a roof since 1826. The unroofed chancel and Portlester Chapel are being given a face-lift as part of this major project. Next to the church stands another bearing the same name, the Roman Catholic St Audoen's, erected in 1841–7 and one of the last churches to be built in the classical style in Dublin. The sheer scale of this church is best appreciated from Cook Street, where the massive stone walls, penetrated by windows only near the top, dominate the streetscape.

HILL STREET
Formerly Temple Street Lower, it was renamed rather unimaginatively by the City Corporation in 1887 because of the bad reputation it had acquired.

HOEY'S COURT
Named after Sir John Hoey, who developed houses on the site. Jonathan Swift was born at No. 7, the home of his uncle, but this is now a barren cul-de-sac leading to an unemployment exchange.

HOLLES STREET
Named after Denzille Holles, Earl of Clare, it is best known for what is officially called the National Maternity Hospital but is

more popularly known simply as 'Holles Street'. Occupying most of the street, this was founded as the South Dublin Lying-in Hospital in 1883 and was built on the site of the former Antrim House. Among those born here was the writer Brendan Behan (1923–64).

HUBAND BRIDGE

Crosses the canal at Mount Street Upper. It is named after Joseph Huband, a director of the Grand Canal Company in 1791.

HUME STREET

Gustavus Hume, a surgeon who speculated in building, was responsible for laying out both Hume Street and Ely Place. Hume Street was the site of one of the definitive conservation battles in Dublin in the 1970s, when students and activists occupied houses at St Stephen's Green in protest at the proposed sale of state-owned property to private developers. They were unsuccessful in their attempts to save the two houses concerned, and reproductions – office buildings – were constructed on the site. Most of the remainder of the houses in Hume Street have been restored. The façade of the Dublin Skin and Cancer Hospital on the southern side of the street is only part of the original intention to continue the central façade treatment along the length of the street.

INFIRMARY ROAD

Named by the Artisans' Dwellings Company in 1886 after the nearby Military Infirmary designed by James Gandon and built in 1787.

INNISFALLEN PARADE

Named after 'sweet Innisfallen', an island on the lower lake of Killarney. Named as part of a pattern in this area based on popular beauty spots and places in Co. Kerry. As a child, the writer Seán O'Casey lived for a time at No. 9, during which his father died.

INNS QUAY

Named after the King's Inns of Court which has occupied a site here since its foundation in 1561 (originally in the cloisters of St Saviour's Abbey, which was closed with the dissolution of the monasteries). This entire quay is given over to the Four Courts and judicial offices. The name refers to the four branches of the common law in Ireland: Chancery, King's Bench, Exchequer and Common Pleas.

The Four Courts – a landmark in Dublin, with its large drum and shallow dome visible the length of the Liffey quays – was constructed between 1786 and 1802. The original plan of the western block designed by Thomas Cooley consisted of a number of separate 'houses', each with its own entrance and stairwell. The eastern block designed by Gandon was one building with one staircase and circulation corridors. This can be seen in plan with Cooley's block on the left. The principal features of the building are the dome and main portico. The portico and pediment barely project from the main mass of the central block, Gandon having created a semi-circular recess under the pediment to bring the entrance into the building. As with all Gandon's important public buildings, the Four Courts was completed by impressive works of sculpture by Edward Smyth. On the main pediment, Moses is flanked by Justice and Mercy, with Wisdom and Authority also present. Trophies of arms are placed over the triumphal arches in the arcades but they have lost some of their grandeur with the crowns replaced by balls.

In the early 19th century the solid parapet wall was removed and replaced with a cast-iron balustrade with the aim of embellishing the surroundings of the Four Courts. It was also suggested at one stage that a bridge should be built on the central axis of the buildings, with a new street cutting through from High Street down to Merchant's Quay. This was never followed through because of public opposition.

Destroyed during the Civil War in 1921–2, the building has since been restored externally and remodelled and rearranged internally. The only external change was the removal of one bay from each of the side blocks so that they no longer project beyond the arcades as originally intended by Gandon. The interior was reconstructed, but the central rotunda remains as Gandon designed it with the four main courtrooms opening off it diagonally. This dramatic public space soars up into the drum creating a sombre and awe-inspiring setting for the administration of the law.

ISLAND STREET

In Rocque's map of 1756, this was known as Dunghill Lane, but it was later renamed for its proximity to Usher's Island. It probably marked the southern boundary of the island before the watercourses were filled in.

ISLANDBRIDGE

So named because of its position at the junction of the Camac and Liffey rivers. Until 1922 this was known as Sarah Bridge, after the Countess of Westmoreland, wife of the Lord Lieutenant at the time of its construction in 1791.

JAMES'S STREET

Named after St James's Church and St James's Gate, one of the old city gates which was also sited in this area. Now best known for the world-famous Guinness brewery. Founded in 1759, it covers over sixty-four acres and is one of the largest breweries in the world.

JERVIS STREET

Named after Sir Humphrey Jervis (1630–1707), Lord Mayor of Dublin in 1681–3, who laid out the area around St Mary's Abbey after buying much of this estate in 1674. Jervis developed a network of streets including Jervis Street, Stafford Street (now Wolfe Tone Street) and Capel Street, as well as building Essex Bridge.

JOHN DILLON STREET

Skilfully detailed, the little houses on this street were designed by Charles Ashworth and built around 1886 on an awkward sloping site as one of the projects of the Artisans' Dwelling Company. The street is named after the 'Young Irelander', John Blake Dillon (1814–66), who founded *The Nation* newspaper along with Charles Gavan Duffy and Thomas Davis. Educated at Trinity College, he joined the Repeal Association in 1841. He was an advocate of a bloodless revolution based on moral force, but changed his mind after the conviction of John Mitchel, deciding that a rising was the only course of action. He escaped to America and only returned after the amnesty of 1855. He was elected MP for Tipperary in 1865 but died suddenly the following year.

Dillon's son John (1851–1927) was an MP for Tipperary from 1880 to 1883, and for East Mayo from 1885 to 1918. A central tenet of his political beliefs was anti-landlordism, which often led to clashes with Parnell. He became leader of the anti-Parnellites in 1896 before the reunification of the Home Rule Party under Redmond in 1900. At the centre of the Home Rule negotiations, he bitterly opposed the British decision to execute the leaders of the 1916 rising.

JOHN MCCORMACK BRIDGE

Opened across the Tolka river in 1984 to link to a new road, Alfie Byrne Road, through reclaimed land in Fairview. The bridge is named after the renowned Irish tenor Count John McCormack (1884–1945).

JOHN'S LANE / STREET

John's Lane East is a pedestrian way along the north side of Christ Church Cathedral, named after the former St John's Church in Fishamble Street, which was first mentioned in 1178 and was demolished in 1884. Although they wind around the rear of the Church of Saints Augustine and John in Thomas Street, John's Lane West and John's Street West were named after the Church of St John-outside-Newgate, first mentioned in 1177.

JONES ROAD

Developed by Frederick E. Jones in 1799 to facilitate travel to and from his theatre in Crow Street. It is now best known for the grounds of the Gaelic Athletic Association, acquired by the GAA in 1913 and named Croke Park after Bishop Thomas Croke.

KELLY'S CORNER

The junction of Camden Street and Harrington Street takes its name from James J. Kelly, City Sheriff and tobacco grower. His National Tobacco Company had offices nearby at 35–36 Camden Street.

KENMARE PARADE

A street of small houses named to a pattern in the area which is based on places of scenic beauty in Co. Kerry.

KEVIN STREET

Kevin Street was originally called St Kevin's Port because of its proximity to St Kevin's Gate, which led to the Liberty of St Sepulchre. There is a pattern of nomenclature in the area based on the name Kevin, after St Kevin's Church. The palace of St Sepulchre, now part of Kevin Street Garda Station, was built as the residence of the Archbishop of Dublin in 1211. The antiquity of the building is still recognisable. It has two fine 17th century gate piers. The name of the street became shortened over the years, and it is now divided into Kevin Street Upper and Kevin Street Lower. It is best known today for the college (1968) of the Dublin Institute of Technology designed by Hooper and Mayne. Another building worthy of note is the small former Moravian Church dating from 1905, designed by O'Callaghan and Webb – a fine pedimented stone building with a small meeting house to the rear. Also on Kevin Street is the Deanery of St Patrick's Cathedral, built in 1781.

KILDARE STREET / PLACE

Originally part of the Molesworth fields or 'lands of Tib and Tom', Kildare Street was known as Coote Lane and then Coote Street until 1753. It was later renamed after the Fitzgeralds, Earls of Kildare and Leinster, who built Leinster House as their townhouse in 1745. The twentieth Earl, James Fitzgerald, first Duke of Leinster, was warned by his friends against building a townhouse in the 'country'. He was sufficiently sure of his position in the social life of the city, however, to predict that fashionable society would take his example. When reminded that he was building in an unfashionable area, he remarked, 'They will follow me wherever I go.' His new house designed by Richard Cassels was described by Thomas Malton in 1794 as, 'the most stately private edifice in the city'. Moreover Fitzgerald was right: within twenty years Merrion Square was being developed and buildings surrounded his home. The house remained in the family for seventy years until it was acquired by the Royal Dublin Society. It was bought from the RDS by the Irish Government in 1925, and is now the seat of the two houses of the Irish Parliament – the Dáil and the Seanad.

Leinster House is clearly a country house. It is of Ardbraccan limestone, with the east or garden front in granite. The east front is a happier design than the west, being plainer and built with warmer material. The projecting bow on the northern side of the house facing the National Library, is said to be the prototype for the bow-fronted White House in Washington. (The architect of the White House was James Hoban, 1762–1832, who studied architecture at the Dublin Society's School (subsequently the Royal Dublin Society), where he won a prize in 1780.) Originally the building had two small wings but these have been replaced with the large blocks of the National Library and the National Museum. The interiors of the building are fairly intact, with the Seanad or Upper House located in the bow-fronted library, while the Dáil sits in a lecture room built by the Royal Dublin Society.

Richard Cassels (1690–1751), the architect of Leinster House, was of German origin and was also known as Richard Castle. He settled in Ireland around 1728 and worked with Edward Lovett Pearce on the Houses of Parliament before becoming the leading country-house architect of his day in Ireland. He was responsible for some of the largest houses in the country including Russborough House (1742–55) in Co. Wicklow, which has the longest frontage of any house in Ireland, and Carton House (1739–45) in Co. Kildare. He was also accredited with Summerhill, Co. Meath, an enormous house burnt in the Civil War in 1922 and finally demolished in the middle of the 20th century – although this may have been designed or at least outlined by Pearce before his death, with Cassels being the executant architect.

Besides Leinster House, Cassels' major works in Dublin were Tyrone House (1740–45) for the Beresfords, and the Rotunda Hospital (1757), which was based on a country-house composition. His dining hall at Trinity College was demolished after the foundations collapsed twice; it was replaced in the 1760s by a building designed by Hugh Darley. Cassels' first independent work in Dublin was the 'printing house', also at Trinity – a little building with a Doric temple front, unusual for Cassels in that the columns are truly free-standing, while his other works had frontispieces of engaged columns or pilasters. It is possible that Pearce did preliminary work for this design, as it was completed only a year after his death. Cassels' work conforms to English Palladianism of the period without betraying any hints of his foreign origins.

Flanking Leinster House are the National Museum of Ireland and the National Library, both designed by Thomas Newenham Deane and his son Thomas Manley Deane, following a competition held in 1885. The addition of a dramatic portico to the west front of Leinster House was originally part of this scheme, but never carried out. The Library has suffered over time, and the original Mountcharles sandstone was replaced after serious erosion. The exterior is characterised by an array of columns and pilasters in the Corinthian order, and by the entrance rotunda – the building's most impressive feature – with its open veranda and corner pavilions framing the composition. Inside, an impressive staircase leads to the magnificent reading room with its vast vaulted ceiling.

The National Museum has recently been undergoing complete restoration inside and out. The elevation to Kildare Street is now cleaned and repaired, showing the brilliance of the sandstone detailing. A much bigger building than the Library, its vast street frontage has a rhythm of large round-headed windows illuminating the exhibition areas. The building suffers from having its secondary entrance and south façade (on Kildare Place) obscured by a partition wall to the rear of government buildings. This façade was originally designed on the basis that Kildare Place would eventually become a larger public space. As with the Library, the corners of the building are expressed using pavilions to frame the composition. The interior is very impressive, with a large entrance hall rotunda and a magnificent central exhibition hall with decorative ironwork and impressive majolica door surrounds. The central gallery has a balcony level and fine staircases.

Amongst the other fine buildings in Kildare Street is one that houses the Department of Enterprise, Trade and Employment formerly the Department of Industry and Commerce. This was the result of a competition announced in 1935 for the design of accommodation for new government departments. The state had been using office space all over the city, and a decision was taken to centralise some of these offices in Kildare Street. J. R. Boyd Barrett won the competition in January 1936 with the present design – basically a stripped classical façade, with the addition of an Art

Deco entrance bay. Construction began in 1939 and finished in 1942. The building has changed little and is a good example of a 1930s public building.

Leaving aside the Art Deco relief sculptures by Gabriel Hayes, the exterior is robust and austere. Although the building is much bigger in mass than those surrounding it, Barrett succeeded in his efforts to ease it into the streetscape by placing a cornice at the prevailing parapet level of the surrounding Georgian houses, and a heavier cornice to mask out the uppermost floor. Other than the cornices and sculptures, the main façade features a regular pattern of window openings. The main emphasis is on the entrance bay at the Schoolhouse Lane corner of the building. A tall round-headed window passes up through the floors with a plain stone surround topped by a carved keystone representing Éire and including jazzy interstitial panels between floors. On the Schoolhouse Lane side, the keystone represents St Brendan the Navigator. Both of the keystones had to be carved in situ. The main entrance is sternly modern in design with heavy cast-bronze gates weighing over one-and-a-half tons. The doorway has a carved lintel depicting the Celtic god Lugh releasing aeroplanes into the air. There are also relief carvings on the balcony of the ministerial office suite. These show stylised images of Industry and Commerce. Apart from this work at Kildare Street, Gabriel Hayes was responsible for a panel on the College of Catering in Cathal Brugha Street called the Mhire Letios. She was also responsible for the designs of the 1p and 2p coins, commissioned in the early 1970s.

The interior of the building remains largely as it was – a single piece of design created by Barrett. It features polished woods and metals, stylised signage and patterned linoleum floors. The foyer for each floor follows a similar design, with deeply coffered ceilings and semi-circular information desks; and black and yellow Art Deco floors with symbols depicting each floor level in the centre. Everything – down to the fireplaces, door handles and even ashtrays – was designed specifically for this building, which was constructed during a time of war and material shortages.

Other fine buildings in Kildare Street include the College of Physicians (1861) designed by William Murray, and the former Kildare Street Club completed in 1861 and designed by Deane and Woodward.

Kildare Place was intended to be a civic space with fine houses off Kildare Street. Unfortunately nothing now remains but the rather forlorn statue of William Conyngham, Baron Plunkett, who was Archbishop of Dublin from 1884 to 1897. One of the houses which once stood here was removed to make way for the National Museum, and two more were dismantled in the 1950s and replaced with the wall to the rear. The remainder were replaced by the Department of Agriculture's building.

KILLARNEY PARADE
Like neighbouring streets, this was named as part of a pattern in the area based on places in Co. Kerry.

KING STREET NORTH
Existing from the 16th century, King Street North was probably named as a foil to nearby Queen Street. It was mentioned as 'King Street, Oxmantown' in 1551 and is probably the 'King's Lane, Oxmantown' referred to in 1438. Located in the Smithfield area, it is currently undergoing redevelopment after years of neglect. In the 17th century it was quite a fashionable street, with stylish houses and a school operated by the Poor Clare nuns for the daughters of wealthy citizens. In 1734 the philosopher and prose writer George Berkeley was consecrated Bishop of Cloyne in St Paul's Church of Ireland.

KING STREET SOUTH
First mentioned in the early 18th century and now best known for

the Gaiety Theatre, one of the few remaining Victorian theatres in Dublin. Designed by C. J. Phipps in the 1860s, the theatre's interior remains almost intact despite a close brush with demolition in the 1970s. Its arcaded polychromic brick façade in a neo-Byzantine style inspired the design of the shopping centre across the street. The Gaiety's bars and levels are still very much as intended, and are warm and cosy when compared with the white and gold rococo fantasy of the main auditorium.

KING'S INNS STREET
In Rocque's map of 1756, this was called Turn Again Lane. Its current name reflects its position near the King's Inns on Henrietta Street.

KINGSLAND PARADE / PARK / AVENUE
Named after the title 'Viscount Kingsland' which became extinct in 1833. Nearby Victoria Street was known as Kingsland Park until 1876.

KIRWAN STREET
Linking Grangegorman to Manor Street, this is called after Dr James Kirwan, Coroner of Dublin, who was a former property owner in the area, in the mid 19th century.

LAMB ALLEY
Takes its name from an inn with a sign depicting the Holy Lamb.

LANGRISHE PLACE
This was named after the Right Honourable Sir Hercules Langrishe (1731–1811), the MP responsible for introducing the Catholic Relief Bill of 1792.

LANSDOWNE ROAD
Named in 1855 after the fourth Marquis of Lansdowne, whose son the fifth Marquis was Governor-General of Canada (1883–8), Viceroy of India (1888–94), Secretary of State for War (1895–1900) and Foreign Secretary (1900–1905). The street is best-known for the Irish rugby football grounds where international rugby and soccer games are played.

LEESON STREET / PLACE / CLOSE
Originally known as Suesey Street, it was renamed in 1728 after the Leesons, Earls of Milltown, who were engaged in brewing. A graceful street lined with Georgian houses (many of them now offices), it is crossed by the Grand Canal which divides it into Leeson Street Upper and Leeson Street Lower.

LEINSTER STREET
Like Nassau Street and Lincoln Place, this was part of St Patrick's Well Lane until 1756. It was renamed for its proximity to Leinster

House, built originally as a large mansion by the Fitzgerald family, Earls of Kildare and Leinster. Facing the park of Trinity College, Leinster Street now consists mainly of commercial premises, with the exception of one fine Georgian house dating from around 1750. Nos. 1-2 once housed Finn's Hotel and Restaurant, where Nora Barnacle was working as a chambermaid when she first met James Joyce in 1904.

LEMON STREET

A narrow street or laneway leading off Grafton Street, it is named after Graham Lemon, a confectioner who owned property here. Previous names include Span's Lane, Grafton Lane and Little Grafton Street.

LENNOX STREET

Charles Lennox, Duke of Richmond and Lord Lieutenant from 1807 to 1813, gave his name to both this street and neighbouring South Richmond Street.

LEO STREET

Named after Pope Leo XIII, elected to the papacy in 1878.

LIBERTY LANE

So named because of its proximity to St Kevin's Gate, the entrance to St Sepulchre's Liberty. Liberty Lane is a narrow winding lane whose country origins show. Originally it extended as far as the canal at Portobello. This route can still be traced, although a warehouse now disrupts it and various sections have been assigned new names.

LIFFEY BRIDGE (THE HA'PENNY BRIDGE)

A symbol of Dublin, the Ha'penny Bridge (officially Liffey Bridge) was opened in 1816. Cast at Coalbrookdale in Shropshire in England, it acquired its popular name from the old halfpenny toll paid to cross the river. It was the only pedestrian bridge on the Liffey until the new Millennium Bridge was opened in 1999. At night it is lit by three lamps supported by curved ironwork above the walkway. Currently badly in need of repair, the bridge moves when crossed and the Corporation now has plans to restore it.

LIFFEY STREET

Named after the river Liffey or 'Anna Livia'. The Liffey rises in the Wicklow mountains and is approximately 110 kilometres long. Running from Benburb Street to Wolf Tone Quay, Liffey Street West originally led straight to the water's edge as there was no quay.

LINCOLN PLACE

Formerly part of St Patrick's Well Lane, then renamed Park Place and later Park Street. Because of the street's bad reputation, in 1862 the Corporation changed its name again, this time calling it after Abraham Lincoln, assassinated President of the United States. British architects Ahrends Burton Koralek have recently extended the Dental Hospital of 1894–96, originally designed by Richard Caulfield Orpen, a half-brother of the noted Irish artist William Orpen. Their sensitive addition in a modern idiom of new laboratories and a landmark tower has been linked to the original building by moving the entrance hall to create a huge, beautiful, well-lit atrium that acts as a central circulation space. Until the 1960s another interesting building on Lincoln Place was the Turkish Baths with its fifty-foot onion dome.

LINDSAY ROAD

Named after the Right Reverend Honourable Charles Lindsay, last Protestant Bishop of Kildare, who died in 1846. The road adjoined his property.

LINENHALL STREET

This was the site of the Linen Hall, which opened in 1728 and closed in 1873. Its business lay principally with certain Ulster towns that were important in the linen industry and are reflected in the names of the adjoining streets: Coleraine Street, Lisburn Street and Lurgan Street. Previously there was also a Derry Street but this was closed to enlarge the Linen Hall in 1781.

LISBURN STREET

Named because of its proximity to Linenhall Street, reflecting the main business of the area by recalling one of the principal towns in Ulster involved in the linen trade.

LITTLE BRITAIN STREET

A narrow continuation of nearby Great Britain Street, now Parnell Street.

LOFTUS LANE

Named after Sir Dudley Loftus (1618–95), the oriental scholar who was buried in St Patrick's Cathedral. In documents dating from 1728 it was mistakenly called Luptus Lane.

LOMBARD STREET EAST / WEST

Named after James Lombard who developed the area along with Sir John Arnott and Edward MacMahon, for whom streets are also named. Lombard Street East was previously called Hervey's Yard and includes the former Peterson's Lane, which ran from City Quay to Townsend Street.

LONG LANE

Named because of its original length, which stretched from New Street to Camden Street. A section of it was renamed Camden Row.

LONGFORD STREET GREAT / LITTLE

Named after Francis Aungier, created Earl of Longford in 1677, who resided here and whose title became extinct in 1704. The Aungiers developed various streets in the area and rebuilt St Peter's Church (since demolished) on lands granted to them in 1621, previously the property of the Carmelite friary.

LOOPLINE BRIDGE

Built between 1888 and 1890 to connect the northbound and southbound railways lines across the Liffey. There was widespread opposition to the bridge, and an appeal was lodged with the Lord Mayor on the grounds that it would obscure the Custom House. This led to a wooden mock-up being constructed. In the end the bridge went ahead despite the opposition, and it does indeed spoil the view of the Custom House from O'Connell Bridge, its metal latticed structure now covered with large advertisements. The labour leader Jim Larkin described the bridge in 1939 as 'the foulest thing that ever disgraced the city'.

LORD EDWARD STREET

Created and opened in 1886 to form a continuous line from Dame Street to Christchurch Place. This resulted in the shortening of Fishamble Street, which had previously extended southwards to Castle Street. When the question of a name for the new street was under debate in the Corporation, alderman Edwin Hamilton suggested 'Street Street' and 'Roe Row' after the architect George Edward Street and whiskey distiller Henry Roe, who were at that time restoring Christ Church Cathedral! Instead, it was named for the patriot Lord Edward Fitzgerald (1763–98), younger son of the first Duke of Leinster. Fitzgerald had served in the English army during the American Revolution but was later to become an admirer of the French Revolution, before being dismissed from the army for toasting the abolition of hereditary titles. He joined the United Irishmen in 1796 and was among those in favour of a militant strategy. He was arrested before the insurrection, thus depriving the organisation of his abilities. Wounded during his arrest, Fitzgerald died shortly afterwards.

LOTTS

Probably refers to the twenty acres of land purchased here and divided into twenty-eight lots by the property developer Humphrey Jervis, who then attempted to lease the lots at ten pounds each.

LUKE STREET

Named after the banker Luke Gardiner who bought land here in 1712. There is also a theory that it may reflect a naming pattern which would connect it to nearby Mark Street.

LUKE KELLY BRIDGE

Formerly known as Ballybough Bridge but renamed after the musician Luke Kelly (1940–84) of 'The Dubliners'.

LURGAN STREET

Like nearby Coleraine Street and Lisburn Street, this is located near the former Linen Hall and was named after the Ulster town which was a centre for the linen industry.

MABBOT LANE
Named after Gilbert Mabbot who built a watermill and millpond here in 1762. He owned property that stretched from Talbot Street to Montgomery Street. Nearby Corporation Street was previously called Mabbot Street.

MACCARTNEY BRIDGE
Crosses the canal at Baggot Street. It is named after John MacCartney, chairman of the Grand Canal Company in 1791.

MACKEN STREET
Previously known as Great Clarence Street after the Duke of Clarence, later William IV (1765–1837).

MACQUAY'S BRIDGE
Crossing the Grand Canal at Grand Canal Street, this is named after George Macquay, a director of the Grand Canal Company in 1791.

MALPAS STREET
It is uncertain whether this was named after Robert Malpas, merchant, who died in 1617, or alderman Patrick Malpas, who died in 1635. Both were buried in St Audoen's Church in High Street. Malpas Street still contains buildings that date from the time when the area was noted for light industry such as weaving and distilling. Several kiln houses survive and have been redeveloped as an enterprise centre.

MALACHI ROAD

Part of a naming pattern in the area based on Norse and Irish history. Malachi refers to the High King Malachi (died 1022) who defeated the Norsemen at Tara in 980 and attacked Dublin three times in 981, 989 and 995.

MANOR STREET

Until 1781 this was included in Stoneybatter. It was named after the manor of Glasnevin and Gorman from which nearby Grangegorman takes its name. The poet Austin Clarke was born at No. 83, which he recalls in the first lines of his poem 'Mnemosyne Lay in Dust'.

> 'Past the house where he was got
> In darkness, terrace, provision shop
> Wing-hidden convent opposite.'

MARK STREET

Named after the nearby church belonging to the parish of St Mark, created in 1708. At times the street has been referred to as St Mark's Street. The church on Pearse Street was built after 1729 but is no longer consecrated. Oscar Wilde was baptised here in 1854.

MARKET STREET SOUTH

A wide cobbled street running between the great brick and stone warehouses of the Guinness brewery, built in 1813 and named after the open and covered markets nearby in the Liberties.

MARLBOROUGH STREET / PLACE

Named after the Duke of Marlborough for his victories in the Wars of the Spanish Succession. In the late 1800s it was briefly known as Tyrone Street after Tyrone House, now occupied by the Department of Education. This was designed by Richard Cassels (or Castle) for Sir Marcus Beresford and was built in 1740. It was bought by the government in 1835, and a replica was constructed beside it to provide extra office accommodation.

MARLBOROUGH STREET is also the location of St Mary's Pro-Cathedral, opened in 1825. The lower part of the street, from Abbey Street to Eden Quay, was formerly a narrow laneway known first as Union Lane or Ferryboat Lane and later as Union Street, but it became part of Marlborough Street early in the 19th century. Another street in the Duke's honour, Blenheim Street, was built to link Talbot Street and Abbey Street. The southern end of Blenheim Street became Northumberland Square in 1844. Much of the site of Blenheim Street and other places adjoining, like the Jewish synagogue (1746) in Marlborough Green, was later absorbed by the large premises of Brooks Thomas and Company. This in turn was developed into the Irish Life Centre and shopping mall. Nothing now remains of either Blenheim Street or Northumberland Square.

MARROWBONE LANE
Possibly derived from St Mary-le-bone.

MARSHALSEA LANE
Originally called Mash Lane, and from around 1793, Marshal Lane. Since 1825 it has been known as Marshalsea Lane after the 'Marshalsea' or debtors' prison which moved here in 1739 from Bridge Street. The debtors were often confined with their families, the majority paying rent for their lodgings to take refuge from their creditors. Robert Emmet used the Marshalsea as an arsenal before it became a barracks for the Dublin militia in the late 1800s. After Independence in 1922 it was used by Dublin Corporation as a tenement. It was demolished in 1975.

MARTIN STREET

Named by the Artisans' Dwellings Company after Sir Richard Martin, City Sheriff in 1886 and Chairman of the ADC.

MARY STREET

Named after St Mary's Abbey (1139) and the parish of St Mary, created in 1697. The Church of St Mary's, designed by Sir William Robinson and opened in 1702, is one of Dublin's finest church buildings, although the exterior is relatively unexciting. Outwardly, the round-headed windows which Robinson also used in the Royal Hospital Kilmainham are the dominant feature. Internally the building is galleried around three sides (it was Dublin's first galleried church), with the organ opposite the main window. The galleries are supported on octagonal columns that also support the roof. The ceiling is barrel vaulted with an elaborate pattern of plasterwork.

The church closed in 1986 and its fate is now uncertain. It has already been used as a home decor store, the shop fittings contrasting incongruously with the galleried interior, stained glass and organ. A proposal exists to convert it to a bar. A new entrance has been knocked out along its northern side, making the southern side, along the adjacent park, the most intact. It is also most demonstrative of Robinson's original design.

Other fine buildings of note in Mary Street include the former Todd Burns department store designed by W. Mitchell and dating from 1905, with its fine façade and large copper dome. This is now Penney's. In 1909 James Joyce opened the Volta Electric Cinema at No. 45, with the backing of some businessmen in Trieste where he was then living. It was Dublin's first cinema, but it did not prosper and was later sold to a group of English businessmen who renamed it The Lyceum.

MARY'S ABBEY

St Mary's was a large Cistercian Abbey founded by the Benedictines in 1139. It was dissolved in the 1530s and then fell into disrepair. The stones from the building were plundered for use elsewhere, some being used in the construction of Essex Bridge.

MARY'S LANE

This has long been the site of Dublin's wholesale fruit market, best observed early in the day when it is invigorated by the hustle of business. It is housed in a building of elegant Victorian steelwork behind façades ornately decorated with representations of the goods being sold within – clumps of onions and other fruit and vegetables, surrounded by terracotta detailing. The sculptures, like those around the granite entrance archways, are by Charles Harrison. The whole ensemble of polychromic brickwork, ornate wrought-iron grilles and sculptures gives the market a note of colour and cheer that is missing in recent buildings of similar purpose around it. Many of the adjacent streets are home to fruit and vegetable warehouses, and the area is a hive of activity. The simpler building opposite was constructed as a fish market.

MATT TALBOT BRIDGE

Named after Matt Talbot (1856–1925), a figure of popular devotion in Dublin who was beatified in 1976 and is best known for his reform from alcoholism to penitence. A firm believer in self-denial, Talbot fasted, remained on his knees for long periods and slept on a plank with a wooden block for a pillow. Upon his death he was found to be wearing chains underneath his clothes as a sign of his slavery to God.

MAY LANE

Named after Charles May who married a daughter of the second Earl of Barrymore.

MAYOR STREET

The street names in this part of the North Lotts are based on a theme reflecting civic institutions and functions: Sheriff Street, Corporation Street, Guild Street and Commons Street are all in the immediate neighbourhood.

MCKENNY'S BRIDGE

Crosses the canal at Lower Mount Street. It is named after Sir Thomas McKenny, a director of the Grand Canal Company in 1791.

MCMAHON STREET

Named after Edward McMahon who, along with Sir John Arnott and James Lombard, developed the area in the 19th century.

MEATH STREET

Once part of the lands of the Abbey of St Thomas à Beckett, and named after William Brabazon, second Baron Ardee, created Earl of Meath in 1627. A busy shopping street for the surrounding residential area, Meath Street has one building of note, St Catherine's Church, designed in 1852 by the leading church architect of his day, J. J. McCarthy. The exterior remains unfinished and has a rather unusual spire and façade.

MEETING HOUSE LANE

So named because of the many religious establishments based in the area in the 17th century – in particular the Presbyterians, who assembled here from 1667 to 1864. In the early 1980s the chapter house of St Mary's Abbey was rediscovered under a bakery, seven feet below street level. It is the sole remaining part of the original abbey complex and dates from 1190. At one time it was possible to lease it for meetings, and it was here, at a meeting of the Privy Council in 1534, that Silken Thomas Fitzgerald initiated his rebellion against King Henry VIII. After hearing of his father's execution, he flung down his sword of state and marched out to raise an army. Subsequently it emerged that his father had not been executed. The chapter house consists of a simple vaulted chamber with single opening Gothic windows in the west façade.

MEETINGHOUSE SQUARE

Meetinghouse Square is one of the new urban spaces created in Temple Bar, accessible from Sycamore Street, Eustace Street, the raised courtyard to the rear of the Irish Film Centre and the short curved street beside the Photographic Archive leading to Rory Gallagher Corner. The Eustace Street entrance continues the pedestrian way formed by the new Curved Street.

The square is used for open-air theatre, music recitals, screenings of films and a weekend food market. It is enclosed by new buildings and surrounded by the Irish Film Centre; the Ark (a children's cultural centre); the Irish Photographic Centre – comprising the Gallery of Photography, the National Photographic Archive and the Dublin Institute of Technology's School of Photography; and a multipurpose building housing the Gaiety School of Acting and a restaurant. A stage situated at the rear of the Ark and a projection room installed in the Photographic Archive ensure that the square is fully utilised on summer evenings.

MELLOWES BRIDGE

The oldest surviving bridge across the river Liffey, named after Lieutenant General Liam Mellowes of the Irish Republican Army who died on 8 December 1922. It was renamed in 1952, having already been renamed as Queen Maeve Bridge in 1922, after the legendary queen of Connaught who invaded Ulster. Built in 1764 and completed in 1768, it was originally known as Queen's Bridge after Charlotte of Mecklenburg, wife of George III. The bridge replaced an earlier structure named Bridewell Bridge, built in 1683.

MEMORIAL ROAD

Named after the Dublin Brigade of 1922, Memorial Road is the continuation eastwards of Beresford Place to the riverbank. Until the early 1920s this area beside the Custom House was the Old Dock, one of the Custom House Docks. It was filled in and the road completed in the early 1950s.

MERCER STREET

Named after Mary Mercer, founder of a hospital for the sick poor which opened here in 1734. The street was previously known as Love Lane but was renamed because of its bad reputation. The hospital was built on the site of the ancient St Stephen's Church and churchyard, and the even older leper hospital. Only the towers and façades of the original Palladian buildings survive, but the Victorian wing with its spiked cupola is a landmark, completing the vista from Merrion Row along St Stephen's Green North and down South King Street. This fine Victorian building designed by J. H. Brett was the result of an architectural competition in 1884.

MERCHANTS ARCH

So named because the archway once passed through the meeting place of the guild of merchants, which was built here in 1822, although the right of way predates this. Many of the guilds were also named after religious figures, this one being known as the guild of the Holy Trinity. Designed by Frederick Darley (1798–1873), the building contains a large room or hall on the upper floor where meetings were held. He also designed the Kings Inns Library and the New Square at Trinity College Dublin.

MERCHANTS QUAY

In medieval times there were slips here to facilitate the loading and unloading of merchant ships. The quay is the site of the church known as 'Adam and Eve's', so called because the original church on the site was hidden behind a public house of that name, through which it was entered. The neo-classical church designed by Patrick Byrne was built in 1834 but was subsequently altered, the campanile having been added in 1923 and the dome in 1959. Only the main west façade remains intact. The church is now screened from the quayside by a building in an Italianate style belonging to the Franciscans.

MERRION ROW

Developed by the Fitzwilliam Estate and named after the second Viscount Fitzwilliam of Merrion. It is a narrow street linking St Stephen's Green to Lower Baggot Street, and is chiefly known for the Huguenot graveyard.

MERRION SQUARE

The first project of the Fitzwilliam estate was Merrion Street, which was quickly built up and followed by plans to develop Merrion Square, using Merrion Street as one side. The square was designed in 1752 by James Ensor, the planner for Rutland Square (now Parnell Square). It was designed to be 1,500 feet long, but as built measured 1,150 feet long and 650 feet wide. The positioning of exit streets at the corners of the square laid the plan for the rest of the estate, which included Mount Street Upper and Mount Street Crescent as well as Fitzwilliam Street. Fitzwilliam Street formed the eastern side of both Merrion Square and (later) Fitzwilliam Square, and was a long expanse of Georgian architecture terminated by Holles Street Maternity Hospital. Holles Street itself was designed to run from the corner of Merrion Square, but it was moved to allow for the building of Antrim House on what is now the site of the hospital.

MERRION SQUARE is perhaps the finest of Dublin's Georgian squares, having escaped the fate of dereliction that befell so much of the Georgian north side of the city, and it has remained intact, unlike St Stephen's Green. It now consists mainly of office accommodation, but some of the fine houses are still residential and most have preserved their interiors and plasterwork.

Among the monuments in the public park at the centre of the square is the Rutland Memorial, built as a drinking fountain in 1791 and commemorating Charles Manners, fourth Duke of Rutland and Lord Lieutenant in 1784–7. At one stage it was proposed to build a national Roman Catholic cathedral on the site of the park, but thankfully the idea was dropped.

No. 1 Merrion Square was the childhood home of Oscar Wilde. The American College now occupies the house where he lived with his father, Sir William R. W. Wilde, the eminent oculist and antiquary, and his mother, the poet 'Speranza'. A statue commemorating the writer, who was born in nearby Westland Row, faces the house from a corner of the park.

Other famous residents of Merrion Square have included Daniel O'Connell (No. 58), Joseph Sheridan Le Fanu (No. 70), sculptor Andrew O'Connor (No. 77), Nobel Prize-winner for Physics Erwin Schrodinger (No. 65) and William Butler Yeats (No. 82). No. 14 was the residence of Sir Philip Crampton, Surgeon General, who was once awoken from his sleep by a messenger reporting that a great personage had fallen from his horse in St Stephen's Green. On arriving there, Crampton found that a gunpowder attack directed at an equestrian statue of King William had blown the figure of the King from his charger!

The western side of Merrion Square is largely given over to the Natural History Museum and the National Gallery of Ireland, which are separated by Leinster Lawn and the garden frontage of Leinster House. The Natural History Museum is a single large block with blank niches set into its long sides. Although externally well designed in a style of austere granite classicism dating from 1856–7, it is the interior that deserves most attention. Known as the 'Dead Zoo', it stands as a living monument to the Victorian museum itself, since its layout and method of display have not changed for over a century. Inside, the ground floor is given over to large Irish animals including two Irish Elks. The upper gallery is a magnificent galleried space with three levels set around an atrium. The galleries are all constructed of cast iron and are reached by two staircases set along the walls. No museum in Dublin contains so many exhibits in such a restricted space.

The exterior of the Natural History Museum gives an idea of the original appearance of the National Gallery, since the elevation of the gallery, designed by Frederick Clarendon, was an exact copy of the museum. After a quarrel with the Board of Trustees, the engineer who acted as architect for the gallery, Griffith, was replaced by Charles Lanyon, who designed the magnificent interior staircase leading from the sculpture gallery. Francis Fowke then replaced Lanyon, and the galleries created by Fowke were so technologically advanced with regard to lighting and ventilation that the National Gallery was considered to be one of the most advanced in Europe. Sir Thomas Manly Deane, who designed the porch, further extended the gallery in 1904. Later extensions were added in 1969 and a restoration programme was started in 1989. Plans are advanced for a new extension on nearby Clare Street.

The statue in front of the National Gallery commemorates William Dargan (1799–1867), the railway engineer.

MERRION STREET

The first project of the Fitzwilliam estate, it was laid out to run parallel to Kildare Street and back on to the gardens and garden frontage of Leinster House, home of the Earls of Kildare. The street narrows at the top where it meets Merrion Row and Lower Baggot Street – a typical occurrence in Dublin, where there was no cohesive planning between the various estates and land owners. Merrion Street was originally a street of large houses, larger than many of those in Merrion Square. On the eastern side, some have recently been restored, amalgamated and converted to become a hotel. One of these, No. 24, was the birthplace of Arthur Wellesley, later the Duke of Wellington.

Across the street is Government Buildings, one of the most visually impressive complexes in Dublin (although this did not prevent it from becoming the butt of many jokes after its expensive restoration and refurbishment in 1990). Built as a college of science, the building had a long construction period. The foundation stone was laid by Edward VII in 1904, the Georgian houses on the site were demolished in 1913 and the building was finally completed in 1922 after the end of British rule in Ireland. The architect was Sir Aston Webb, although credit is usually also given to Thomas Manly Deane, whose offices were demolished for the building but who played little part in the project.

The building is constructed around a courtyard, with the central dome placed over the pedimented central block to the rear of the site. Unlike many of Dublin's domed buildings, the dome is lead-clad, not copper, and is left visible to the street by the use of a columned screen and gateway. Atop the flanking blocks on Merrion Street are large sculptures depicting the sciences.

MESPIL ROAD

Like nearby Morehampton Road and Pembroke Road, Mespil Road, running alongside the Grand Canal, is named after the seventh Viscount Fitzwilliam who inherited the estates of the eleventh Earl of Pembroke. It is a street of mixed usage, with several office blocks at the Baggot Street end while the other end still has the large residential houses that were once very fashionable but are now mainly office conversions. The songwriter Percy French (1854–1920) once lived at No. 35, which is marked by a plaque to commemorate him.

MILL STREET

Named after two mills belonging to the Abbey of St Thomas, which was granted to Sir William Brabazon in 1538 along with most of this area.

MILITARY ROAD

So named because it leads from the Royal Hospital Kilmainham to the military barracks at Islandbridge. The Royal Hospital is a mile-and-a-half west of the city centre; at the time of its construction the site was part of the Phoenix Park. Designed as a home for invalid soldiers by Sir William Robinson when it opened in 1684, it was the first major public building in Dublin since medieval times. It was seen at the time as an important and impressive construction, and one commentator even suggested that the hospital and the university (Trinity College) could exchange buildings! After lying empty for many years, the Royal Hospital has now been refurbished and is in use again as the Irish Museum of Modern Art (IMMA).

The building consists of four unbroken ranges enclosing a courtyard, and was based on Les Invalides in Paris. It is similar to Les Invalides in its purpose – the provision of accommodation for old soldiers – and in the adoption of a closed courtyard plan with arcaded walks corresponding to passages on the floors above. Two years after construction was started Wren began building for a similar purpose at Chelsea. The northern side of the building contains the dining hall and chapel and is marked by the clock tower and spire. The chapel is expressed externally by the large stained-glass window that breaks through the main cornice of the building. The ranges are two storeys in height with a further dormer storey. The tower can be seen from quite a distance away and is positioned outside the main structure, breaking through the roof of the pedimented entrance to the great hall. It has three stages, the base, an octagonal stage and the spire, which has handles much like those placed by James Gibbs at St Martin-in-the-Field's in London in 1722–6. Here Robinson was doing this as early as 1701.

The interiors of the building were largely destroyed when the building was converted for use as an art gallery but the chapel and main hall are still intact. The chapel is finely carved in oak by the immigrant Huguenot craftsman James Tarbury. The main window has a fine wooden surround with tiers of classical columns. The ceiling was replaced in Victorian times and is made of papier-mâché rather than fine plaster as it appears. It is a hugely elaborate work with cherubs and angels. The dining room, centrally situated along the right hand side in plan, is a more restrained room. Of huge proportions, its only decoration is a prominent cornice and portraits of former Lord Lieutenants. The remainder of the interiors were less elaborate, but an impressive series of vaults survives below.

For a time the quadrangle was used to store old statues of British monarchs which had been removed from public spaces around Dublin after Independence. A statue of Queen Victoria, previously in place in front of Leinster House, was stored here for many years before finally being sold to the city of Victoria in Australia. A new foyer and bookshop constructed within the external fabric of the old building contains a magnificent glass and steel staircase. The series of arcades around the quadrangle give the building a monastic air, making it an ocean of calm within the city.

MILLENNIUM BRIDGE

A new pedestrian bridge across the Liffey which opened in late 1999. It is located approximately half-way between Grattan Bridge and the Ha'penny Bridge, and links Lower Ormond Quay on the north bank of the river with Wellington Quay.

MISERY HILL

In the early 13th century, there was a leper hospital close to the junction of modern Townsend Street and Hawkins Street. Sufferers who were unable to gain entrance to the hospital would spend the night at Misery Hill, well away from the town and its citizens. This was also where the corpses of those hanged at Gallows Hill were sometimes left to hang for anything up to twelve months.

MOLESWORTH STREET

This area was originally known as Molesworth Fields. The street was laid out by Richard, third Viscount Molesworth, who had several houses in Dawson Street removed so that the two streets could be made to intersect. In 1978 St Anne's School and Molesworth Hall at the junction of Dawson Street and Molesworth Street were demolished to be replaced by an office block.

One of the most important buildings remaining on the street is the Masonic Hall, completed in 1866 on the site of the townhouse of the first Grandmaster, the Earl of Rosse. The result of an architectural competition, it was designed by Edward Holmes of Birmingham. The façade is unusual for Dublin. The architect used three classical orders: Doric, Ionic and Corinthian. The pediment contains the Masonic square and compass. The interior is a riot of colour, architectural styles and themes. The Royal Arch chapter room has an Egyptian theme; the Prince Mason's chapter room is Gothic Tudor, and the Knights Templar room is designed as a medieval chapel.

MOLYNEAUX YARD

From the Molyneaux family whose home was located here until Thomas Molyneaux built Molyneaux House, near Peter Street, in 1711.

MONCK PLACE

Named after the Monck family, local landlords and Earls of Rathdowne.

MONTPELIER HILL

For a short time in the 19th century Montpelier Hill was the site of the residence of a Royal Duke, the Duke of Cambridge, at that time Prince George of Cambridge, grandson of George III and first cousin of Queen Victoria. He was stationed in Dublin as an officer in the army and member of the Dublin garrison. He afterwards commanded the Dublin District garrison, served in the Crimea and was Commander-in-Chief of the British Army for many years. He lived here for a very short time, his residence for the greater part of his stay in Dublin being his quarters in the Royal Barracks. While in Dublin he was married in Arbour Hill garrison church to Miss Louisa Farebrother, an actress. As the marriage was contracted without the consent of the sovereign, Queen Victoria, it was contrary to the Royal Marriage Act, passed in the reign of George III at the King's wish. The marriage was therefore always regarded as morganatic or an unequal marriage. The couple's eldest son did not succeed to the title of Duke of Cambridge.

MOORE STREET

Developed by Henry Moore, Earl of Drogheda, and one of many streets in the area bearing his name. It is best known for its fruit and vegetable market.

MOSS STREET

Possibly a reference to the nearby mill complex originally built for Bewley, Moss and Company, sugar refiners.

MOUNT STREET LOWER / UPPER

Probably named after the mound of Gallows Hill. This lay

between here and modern Baggot Street, which is shown in Rocque's map of 1756 as Gallows Road. Confusingly, Lower Mount Street and Upper Mount Street are near each other but do not meet or intersect. Lower Mount Street has lost most of its graceful houses to large office developments. Over sixty houses have been demolished in the street in the last few decades.

UPPER MOUNT STREET opens into Mount Street Crescent, at the centre of which stands St Stephen's Church, better known to Dubliners as the Pepper Canister because of its distinctive spire. Started in 1821, it was designed by John Bowden and completed by the architect Joseph Welland of the First Fruits Board after his death. The rear and side of the building are treated simply with round-headed windows and a circular apse. Most of the design work was reserved for the front, where the magnificent vista from Leinster House along the south side of Merrion Square ends. The façade has a simple unadorned pediment supported by two central Doric columns. Above this breaks the pepperpot spire, with its familiar copper-clad dome. The stern entrance is exaggerated by an overly tall doorway. St Stephen's is still in use for services and occasionally for concerts and recitals.

MOUNTJOY SQUARE

This was named after Luke Gardiner, first Viscount Mountjoy (Earl of Blessington), who developed the square. He was the grandson of Luke Gardiner who had built Henrietta Street. Mountjoy Square is the only true square in Dublin, measuring 600 feet long by 600 feet wide, and it was designed as a single symmetrical scheme with a church in the centre. The original plans show symmetrical terraces of houses with uniform façades. The terraces were to have central cupolas and domed pavilions at the ends. These were not built and the ubiquitous elevation was adopted.

Two streets exit the square at each corner. One of them, Mountjoy

Place, is a short cul-de-sac created for the purpose of completing this arrangement. The streets going north-south run straight through the square, while those running east-west are offset by two houses to allow corners to be formed confirming the space. It was not possible to achieve unity between Mountjoy Square and the other holdings of the Gardiner estate around Rutland Square (now Parnell Square) because the land in between – including North Great Georges Street – was owned by another family. In the 20th century Mountjoy Square became very run down and many houses were demolished because they were unsafe. In recent years, these gaps have been filled in with pastiche houses, allowing the square to recover some of its past appearance.

MUCKROSS PARADE

Like many of the narrow streets near here, Muckross Parade is named after a beauty spot in Co. Kerry.

MURTAGH ROAD

Named, like other streets in the area, according to a pattern based on Irish and Norse history which included the names of Irish kings.

NASSAU STREET / PLACE

Until it was renamed in the 1700s after the Royal House of Nassau, this was known as St Patrick's Well Lane from a 12th century well that dried up in 1729. According to the legend, St Patrick struck the ground with a staff and brought water bubbling to the surface. When the Thingmote, the Viking earthen mound used for assemblies, was demolished in 1685, the earth from it was used to raise the street by eight feet to prevent it from flooding. In 1842 the level of the high wall of Trinity College, which runs along the north side of the street, was lowered and surmounted by railings still in place today.

The old Library of Trinity College ('old' because of its newer neighbour, built by Ahrens Burton Koralek) was designed by Thomas Burgh and is his masterpiece. A huge building, it towered over the university and city when completed. Even today, surrounded as it is by similarly scaled buildings, it is still imposing, dominating the view of the university from Nassau Street. The building has undergone two major adaptations. Originally the Library was placed over an open ground floor arcade whose purpose was to insulate the books from damp. This arcade was filled in during the 19th century to provide for more shelf space. The Library originally had a high flat ceiling, the timber tunnel vaults that cap it having been added by Deane and Woodward in 1858–60. They were also responsible for the mansard roof.

Another fine building in the university that can be seen from Nassau Street is the former museum designed by Deane and Woodward. The winning design in a competition for a museum and lecture hall complex for Trinity in 1852, this was one of the first statements in architecture of the pre-Raphaelite ideals. A palazzo-style structure with Lombardesque detailing, the museum is highly decorated, with over 180 different carved capitals. The most impressive part of the building is the area of the hallway and staircases. The columned hallway leads into a double-domed chamber, with a dividing staircase leading into two Byzantine arcades. At one time there was a plan to have the interior decorated with frescos by Rossetti. Many of the interiors designed for the building by Deane and Woodward were never executed, because the college's resident architect John McCurdy persuaded the board of the university against them. Many of those visible today are therefore rather poor efforts designed by McCurdy.

NELSON STREET

In common with nearby Wellington Street, this was named to commemorate a famous military figure, Admiral Nelson. Like London, Dublin erected a column in Nelson's honour, but the Irish monument was blown up in 1966 and nothing remains.

NEW STREET

Originally part of the *Slíghe Chualann*, one the four great roads traversing Ireland that came together in or around Dubh-linn or Áth Cliath. New Street is one of the oldest streets in Dublin, dating from the 13th century, when it was developed as part of St Sepulchre's Liberty. New Row South, which runs parallel to it, was once a centre for the weaving and brewing industries.

NEWCOMEN BRIDGE

Crosses the Royal Canal at North Strand. It is named after Sir William G. Newcomen, a director of the Royal Canal Company in 1791.

NEWMARKET

In 1674 the Earl of Meath applied for permission to operate bi-weekly markets and fairs here. By 1676 the area was developed. The market dealt mainly in country produce and wool for the weavers based in the surrounding streets. Almost the same size as Smithfield market on the north side of the Liffey, Newmarket is a grand civic space and acts as a focus for the surrounding streets. Once a centre for the brewing industry, the area, with its wide marketplace, is now mainly occupied by light industrial units.

NEWPORT STREET

Beside the harbour of the Grand Canal at James's Street, this was the original port of the canal system in Dublin. It was later superseded by the new Grand Canal docks constructed on the South Lotts and behind Sir John Rogerson's Quay, although Guinness continued to use the harbour for many years for transporting stout to the midlands by barge. Although this part of the canal has now been filled in, its path can be traced on maps.

NIALL STREET

One of a number of streets in this area of houses built by the Artisans' Dwellings Company. The streets are named to a pattern based on Irish and Norse history and folklore.

NICHOLAS STREET

Named after the Church of St Nicholas Within, the remains of which can be seen at the corner of the Peace Park on Christchurch Place. The parish of St Nicholas of Myra was divided in two, within and without the city walls. The church was originally built in the mid-12th century and was rebuilt several times before finally being demolished in 1835.

NORSEMAN PLACE

Reflects a naming pattern based on a theme derived from Irish and Norse history, a feature of this area once known as Oxmantown, now Stoneybatter.

NORTH CIRCULAR ROAD

Laid out in 1763 as one of the boundary roads of the city, at a little over three miles long. When opened, it was a fashionable promenade by which to drive to the Phoenix Park. The road still has some fine brick houses, although many have been converted to flats and apartments.

NORTH GREAT GEORGE'S STREET

Named after George III, this was part of the Eccles estate owned by the Archdall family who lived at nearby Mount Eccles. The street presents one of the most intact Georgian streetscapes on the north side of the city, with most of the houses dating from the late 1780s. It was once a very fashionable place to live. Residents have included the poet Sir Samuel Ferguson (1810–86) at No. 20; Lord Kenmare at No. 35; and the Provost of Trinity College, John Pentland Mahaffy (1838–1918) at No. 38. After years of neglect when many houses were used as tenements, the area is gradually returning to its former grandeur, and buildings are undergoing restoration. The James Joyce Centre is at No. 35.

NORTH LOTTS

Rather than denoting a street, this is the name given to the area east of the Custom House and contained southwards by the North Wall Quay, which in 1682 was surveyed and divided into 152 lots, to be awarded by lottery to members of the city assembly and selected officials. In 1686, this process was declared void and was abandoned. In 1717 a committee reported to the assembly with a series of proposals, including the re-routing of the Tolka River. Various streets were laid out, including Sheriff Street, Commons

Street, Guild Street and Mayor Street. The area was divided up into 132 lots, each consisting of two plots facing either the North Wall Quay or one of the new streets.

NORTH WALL QUAY

Built to reclaim the lands known as the North Lotts from the tidal Liffey, the North Wall was for many years the departure point for the Irish Sea steam packets that took so many emigrants away from Ireland. Used for many years mainly as railway freight yards and port facilities, the area is now anticipating a rejuvenation with the expansion of the IFSC (International Financial Services Centre) and related developments as far as Guild Street. The building known today as the Point Depot or Theatre (or simply the Point) was renovated and converted for use as a concert and exhibition venue from its previous function as a railway shed and terminus for the Midland and Great Western Railway Company.

NORTHUMBERLAND ROAD

Named after Hugh Percy, fourth Duke of Northumberland and Lord Lieutenant in 1829–30. Nearby Percy Place is also named after him.

OBSERVATORY LANE

A cul-de-sac off Lower Rathmines Road where a manufacturing works owned by Sir Howard Grubb produced astronomical instruments.

O'CONNELL BRIDGE

O'Connell Bridge was designed and built by James Gandon at the behest of the Wide Streets Commissioners, O'Connell Bridge was completed in 1795 and was originally named Carlisle Bridge after a former Lord Lieutenant, Frederick Howard, Lord Carlisle. This bridge had a hump and was much narrower than the present one, at only forty-three feet wide. It had obelisks and plinths designed by Gandon at the four corners, but in 1804 the obelisks were removed and discussion started about the bridge's inadequate width, its steepness and its state of disrepair. Finally in 1880 it was widened and the hump removed. Of equal width to O'Connell Street, at 45 metres, it is now almost square – as wide as it is long. It was renamed after Daniel O'Connell (1775–1847) in 1880.

O'CONNELL STREET

Originally extending only from present-day Parnell Street to Abbey Street, the street now known as O'Connell Street was first developed by the Moore family, Earls of Drogheda, and was known as Drogheda Street. When Luke Gardiner purchased the land from the Moores in the mid-1700s he demolished the houses on the west side and created a street 1,050 feet long and 150 feet wide. This was laid out with a central mall, fifty feet wide, decorated with obelisks and trees, with a fifty-foot wide roadway on either side of it. It became a fashionable place to live and was lined with large houses. Gardiner originally intended to continue the street to the river and have the vista terminated by a large public building on the south side of the river.

At the northern end, Dr Bartholomew Mosse took a lease on land on Great Britain Street (now Parnell Street) and built the complex known as the Rotunda Hospital and Assembly Rooms. The lack of cohesive planning in Dublin is apparent here, the Rotunda being placed not on the axis of Sackville Street (the new name given to the greater part of Drogheda Street after it had been widened and developed by Gardiner), but to one side, thus allowing the Assembly Rooms to terminate the vista from the other end of the street. In Rocque's map of 1756, Sackville Street ends at Henry Street, with the name Drogheda Street now applying only to the much narrower portion of the street that continued on to meet Abbey Street. Later, in 1785, the Wide Streets Commissioners decided to extend Sackville Street to the river and to construct a bridge (where none had existed previously) to connect it with two new streets – D'Olier Street and Westmoreland Street. The bridge opened in 1795 while work was still ongoing on the Sackville Street extension. After Independence the street was renamed O'Connell Street after 'the Liberator', Daniel O'Connell (1775–1847).

The central mall of O'Connell Street contains statues to various people who have played a role in the development of Dublin or Ireland. Dominated by the O'Connell monument, they include Sir John Gray (1816–75), for his efforts in bringing the Vartry water supply to Dublin in 1868; Fr Theobold Mathew, founder of the temperance movement (1790–1856); William Smith O'Brien, one of the 'Young Irelanders' (1803–64); and James Larkin (1876–1947), labour leader and trade unionist.

The O'Connell monument was erected after a subscription list was opened in 1862. Two years later a competition was announced but none of the entries met with the approval of the committee. After a second unsuccessful competition, it was decided to invite the leading sculptor of the day, John Henry Foley (1818–74), who was then working on the Albert Memorial in London, to undertake the project. Foley died before it was completed, and his assistant finished the work. The monument is in three parts. The base is heavy limestone, with four winged figures representing Patriotism, Fidelity, Courage and Eloquence. Above this is a drum surrounded by figures representing O'Connell's labours and triumphs, while surmounting the entire monument is the figure of the man himself.

At the other end of O'Connell Street stands the monument to Charles Stewart Parnell, commissioned in 1900 and completed in 1910 to the design of the Dublin-born American sculptor Augustus Saint Gaudens. In complete contrast to the O'Connell monument, this consists of a simple triangular obelisk topped by a bronze flame, with Parnell's likeness standing at the foot of the obelisk.

The GPO or General Post Office is situated at the centre of the western side of O'Connell Street. Built in 1814 and designed by Richard Johnston, it holds a special place in Irish history as the focal point of the Easter rising of 1916 and the spot where the Proclamation of the Republic was read out. The building was gutted in the ensuing battle, as was most of Lower O'Connell Street. Inside, a statue of the Irish mythical hero Cúchulainn (by Oliver Shepherd) commemorates the events that took place here. The GPO's main feature is the huge Doric portico above the pavement, spanning the five central bays. The cornice is heavily carved and topped by a huge dentil frieze and balustrade, recently replaced. To each side of the portico are five further bays. Above are statues by John Smyth representing Hibernia, with Fidelity and Mercury on either side.

In the centre of O'Connell Street, facing the GPO, stood the famous Nelson Pillar, which was blown up in the 1960s. The foundation stone for this column to the memory of Admiral Nelson was laid by the Duke of Richmond, Lord Lieutenant, on 5 February 1808. The monument, 134 feet high, was erected the same year at a cost of £6,858, raised by public subscription. It was designed by William Wilkins of Norwich, although the statue of Nelson at the top of the column was the work of an Irish sculptor, Thomas Kirk. The monument was blown up in the middle of the night in March 1966, but the head of Nelson has been preserved by the Dublin Civic Museum. A recent proposal is to build a replacement monument on this site, a stainless steel spike 120 metres high, designed by Ian Richie Architects.

O'DONOVAN ROSSA BRIDGE
Built in 1813 and opened in 1816, this was originally known as Richmond Bridge after a Viceroy of this name, but it was renamed in 1922 after Jeremiah O'Donovan Rossa (1839–1915), a leading republican and Fenian. O'Donovan Rossa founded a literary and political group, the Phoenix Society, which was later associated with the Fenian movement. He was imprisoned between 1856 and 1871 and later directed the first bombing campaign in Britain in the early 1880s. During the building of the bridge, German, Spanish and British coins and weapons were found under the foundations on the south side of the river, while two eighteen-foot boats – in one of which a skeleton was found under the north side. The bridge features keystone heads in the manner of the Custom House on each of its three arches. The elaborate cast-iron and stone balustrade was continued along Inns Quay and Father Mathew Bridge to improve the environs of the Four Courts.

OLAF ROAD
Many of the small streets in this area are named after figures from Irish and Norse history. This one probably recalls Olaf Cuaran

who was defeated by the High King at Tara in 980. Olaf had ruled Dublin and Dyflinnarskiri (the Norse Kingdom of Dublin) since 945. He retired to Iona as a pilgrim after his defeat.

OLIVER BOND STREET

Named after Oliver Bond (1760–98), a prominent woollen merchant who joined the United Irishmen. He was arrested and sentenced to death but died in Newgate prison. The street was formerly part of Mullinahack (from the Irish muileann an chac, a dung mill). Bond's home was near here on Lower Bridge Street.

O'RAHILLY PARADE

Named after Michael O'Rahilly (1875–1916), an associate of Arthur Griffith and a founder member and Director of Arms of the Irish Volunteers. Unaware of the preparations for the 1916 rising, he attempted with Eoin MacNeill to call it off. When this failed he joined in and was killed in the fighting.

ORIEL PLACE / STREET

Oriel was a kingdom in ancient Ireland corresponding roughly to modern Co. Monaghan, and ruled by the MacMahons.

ORMOND QUAY

This is named after James Butler, first Duke of Ormonde (1610–88) and three times Lord Lieutenant of Ireland, who insisted that the houses built on the north bank of the Liffey should face the river. Sir Humphrey Jervis developed Ormond Quay under a lease obtained in 1674. Jervis had originally intended to build the terraces with their backs to the river, but was persuaded by Ormonde to reverse this and leave the street open to the water to form a quay. Nearby Ormond Square was for many years the site of the Ormond Markets.

OXMANTOWN LANE

The name derives from Ostmanstown, to which the Anglo-Normans banished the Vikings in the 12th century who had previously been living within the city walls. They subsequently seemed to make the area their home. Oxmantown was once a village separate from Dublin. It covered the area now occupied by Church Street (the southern end), Smithfield, Bow Street, Queen Street, Blackhall Street, Hendrick Street and the western half of North King Street. The name is derived from the Ostmen or Eastmen, a name given to the Scandinavians, who came from a land lying east of Ireland and England. It recalls a time when Dublin was a Scandinavian kingdom whose kings had such hibernicised names as Sitric MacAuliffe and Hasculph MacTorkill. The name of Ostman Place has the same origin.

PARKGATE STREET

So named because it is near the main entrance (from the city) to the Phoenix Park. In 1786 the Wide Streets Commissioners were given permission to 'alter and widen the road westward from Barrack Street to Island Bridge'. The western end became Conyngham Road; the eastern end was called Park Gate Street. Ryan's pub in Parkgate Street is probably the finest Victorian pub in the city, dating from 1896. It still retains most of its original lay-out and fittings, including engraved mirrors, brass lamps, stained glass panels in the windows, two snugs and a fine central carved oak and mahogany bar.

PARLIAMENT STREET

The development of this thoroughfare was the first project undertaken by the Wide Streets Commissioners. (The Commission was created by an Act of Parliament specifically for the purpose.) The street completes the north-south axis of Capel Street, the vista from that street extending across the river to terminate at City Hall.

Architecturally, Parliament Street's most outstanding feature is Sunlight Chambers, one of the most exuberant buildings in Dublin. It was designed as the Dublin offices of Lord Lever (of the firm of Lever Brothers) by the Liverpool architect Edward Ould, who also designed Port Sunlight, the Lever town and works in England. Built in a romantic Italianate style with its wide overhanging eaves, tiled roof and arcaded upper floors, the building boasts one of the most unusual architectural features in Dublin: two multi-coloured terracotta friezes depicting the history of hygiene. Ironically these friezes had become quite dirty until recently, but the building has now been restored to its original brilliance.

At the time of its construction Sunlight Chambers met with resistance from architects in Dublin because a foreign architect had been hired for the job. (Edwin Lutyens had this problem a few years later with the aborted gallery sponsored by Hugh Lane which was to be built over the Liffey in place of the Ha'penny Bridge.) When the new building was complete, *The Irish Builder* referred to it as the ugliest building in Dublin, and a few years later the same journal called it 'pretentious and mean'.

PARNELL STREET

Parnell Street has been decimated by its widening in the 1980s to provide a dual carriageway from Parnell Square to the top of Capel Street. Formerly known as Great Britain Street, it was renamed on 1 October 1911 following the unveiling of the statue of Charles Stewart Parnell (1846–91). Parnell came from a Protestant land-owning family in Co. Wicklow and was educated at Cambridge. He was Home Rule MP for Meath from 1875 to 1880 and for Cork City from 1880 until his death; and was President of the Irish Parliamentary Party from 1880 onwards. Parnell was a good public speaker, and his tactics inside the House of Commons included that of obstruction in association with J. C. Biggar by making long speeches to delay and prevent votes. His career was ruined however by an affair with a married woman, Katherine O'Shea, and by his subsequent citation as a correspondent in divorce proceedings initiated by her husband in 1889. This resulted in a split in the Home Rule Party. He married Kitty O'Shea shortly before his death.

PARNELL SQUARE

Formerly Rutland Square, this was the second of Dublin's squares. The name originally referred to the park in the centre, which was named after Charles Manners, fourth Duke of Rutland and Lord Lieutenant in 1784–87, who died while in office. The surrounding streets were known as Charlemont Row, Cavendish Row, Palace Row and Great Britain Street. Cavendish Row, renamed from Cavendish Street in 1766, was named after William Cavendish, third Duke of Devonshire and Lord Lieutenant from 1737 to 1745. The centre of the square is now mostly taken over by the Rotunda Hospital and the National Garden of Remembrance. Opened in 1966, the Garden of Remembrance was designed by the architect Dáithí Hanly and features a large sunken pool with mosaics depicting discarded weapons. Over the pool stands a large bronze sculpture by Oisín Kelly, 'The Children of Lir'.

The Rotunda Hospital – officially the Dublin Lying-in Hospital – was the first maternity hospital in Great Britain or Ireland, and at the time of its creation was the largest in the world. It is in fact two separate complexes, the hospital proper and the 'Rotunda' - the rooms created for social purposes, from which the hospital derives its name. The hospital was founded by Bartholemew Mosse (1712–59) in 1745. It was originally situated in Fownes Court off Dame Street, but it was moved by Mosse to its present location in 1748. At that time the site at the top of Gardiner's Mall (the northern end of present-day O'Connell Street) was bordered by open countryside. The design of the hospital by Richard Cassels, a friend of Mosse's, was based on Cassels' design for Leinster House. The composition of the façade is that of a country house, with its wings and curving links. The central block is distinguished by the large window that lights the chapel inside, and by the campanile with its decorative baroque copper dome. The campanile is placed centrally in elevation but is sited to the rear of the block. The most important interior feature of the hospital is the sumptuous chapel, designed with fundraising in mind – perhaps a curious notion today, but charity sermons were then a popular form of entertainment. The chapel was therefore centrally situated above the main entrance at first floor level.

The hospital was totally dependent on charity, and for this reason the building and its environs generally were created with an eye to fundraising. The 'social' rooms of the Rotunda existed to provide entertainment; pleasure gardens surrounded the hospital; and the exterior was designed to attract the attention of fashionable Dublin society. The Rotunda was extended many times from its original design by James Ensor, with later additions by Richard Johnston and James Gandon. While the exterior is relatively undistinguished for a building that 'closes' such an important vista (it is visible the length of what is now O'Connell Street), the interior was regarded as having one of the finest circular rooms in Britain. The 'Round Room' is now the Ambassador Cinema, the former 'Supper Rooms' are the Gate Theatre and the 'Pillar Room' underneath the theatre is occasionally used for concerts. The sculpted stone frieze around the exterior of the Round Room and the entrance block to the theatre are the work of James Gandon. The curving wings that link the smaller blocks to the main body of the hospital create some interesting public spaces - the bar of the Gate Theatre is an example.

On the northern side of Parnell Square is the Hugh Lane Gallery of Modern Art, previously the Dublin Municipal Art Gallery. This was originally the home of Lord Charlemont, which gave its name to Charlemont Row. Completed in 1763, the house was designed by Sir William Chambers, whom Lord Charlemont had befriended in Italy where Chambers was studying Roman antiquities and Charlemont was on a collecting trip. Years later Charlemont hired him to design the building known as the Casino on his family estate at Marino outside Dublin. He turned to him again when his need arose to have a residence in the city. Consisting of a single block of five bays with curved screen walls to either side, the house breaks up the regularity of this side of Parnell Square, being set back from the other houses. The original ground floor (now destroyed) had a central vestibule with a staircase set in a curved bay. There was also a long gallery and pavilion designed to hold Charlemont's large and important collection of books and antiquities. The space between the pavilion and the main house has now been filled by galleries.

Charlemont's extravagant collecting and building left his estate in financial difficulties, and his successor, the second Earl, sold everything but Charlemont House, the Casino and Marino House. The third Earl sold the library, described as the finest private library ever likely to be seen in Ireland, and one of the finest ever put together this side of the Atlantic. Charlemont House was sold to the government in 1870, becoming first the General Register and Census Office, and later the Municipal Gallery, a development of which Charlemont would undoubtedly have approved. Today, on the same side of the square in another fine Georgian house, is the Dublin Writers' Museum.

No. 5 Parnell Square East was the birthplace of Oliver St John Gogarty (1878–1957). Gogarty was a noted surgeon as well as a prominent figure in the literary life of Dublin. A senator of the Irish Free State in 1922, he survived an attempt on his life when he was kidnapped from his home in Ely Place. His best-known work, *As I was Going Down Sackville Street*, was published in 1937. It resulted in a highly publicised libel case which he lost. The damages against him were substantial, and disillusioned with Ireland, he left for the United States, coming back only on visits. He died in New York shortly before his planned return to Ireland. His remains were flown back and buried in Connemara.

PATRICK STREET

Named after St Patrick's Cathedral. The present cathedral was founded by Archbishop John Comyn in 1192, but was built on the site of an earlier church believed to have been established by St Patrick. Tradition had it that a holy well here had been used by the saint for baptisms, and a church existed as early as the late 5th century. A stone marking the site of the well was found in 1901 when nearby buildings were demolished in order to form the park beside the cathedral.

As Archbishop of Dublin, John Comyn had resided in the priory of Christ Church Cathedral. Unwilling to submit to the jurisdiction of the city's provosts, he established another cathedral and a palace outside the city walls. Known as St Sepulchre's, the palace remained the seat of the Archbishops of Dublin until 1806; what remains of it is now part of Kevin Street Garda Station. It is probable that Comyn intended to reduce the status of Christ Church, and its refusal to accept the removal of its privileges produced the anomaly of Dublin having two cathedrals for one diocese. St Patrick's was rededicated in 1254, following a period of rebuilding which began in 1225.

A university was founded at St Patrick's Cathedral in 1320 with the approval of Pope Clement V. This continued in existence until the end of the 15th century when it closed due to lack of funds, although Archbishop Browne tried to revive it in 1547. A fire destroyed the cathedral tower and part of the west nave in 1362. In 1584 Queen Elizabeth I issued an edict 'to consider how a college might be erected' in Dublin. St Patrick's was considered unsuitable and the former Augustinian priory of All Hallows, on what is now College Green, was chosen for the site of Trinity College.

Like nearby Christ Church, the cathedral building was much neglected over the years and by 1860 it was in poor condition.

Again like its neighbour, St Patrick's acquired a wealthy benefactor, Sir Benjamin Guinness, who funded the restoration of the building in the 1860s at a cost of around £160,000. In 1872, as a result of the disestablishment of the Church, St Patrick's became a national cathedral for the Church of Ireland. It is now used by the state for ecumenical services.

St Patrick's is one of the largest cathedrals in Ireland, where cathedrals tend to be smaller than on the continent. It is 91 metres long externally and the nave is 17 metres high. Built in an Early English Gothic style, it has heavy buttressing and stout walls. Internally it is dominated by monuments to important families and individuals associated with the city and the cathedral over its 800-year existence. Many of these are highly ornate; they add to the cathedral's appeal and emphasise its important role in the history of the city. Jonathan Swift, author of *Gulliver's Travels*, was Dean of St Patrick's for many years. His portrait shows the cathedral in the background.

PEARSE STREET

Originally Moss Lane and later Great Brunswick Street, this was eventually named Pearse Street after the brothers Pádraig and Willie Pearse, protagonists in the 1916 Easter rising, who were born here. Great Brunswick Street was originally built to link the Grand Canal Docks with the city centre to facilitate commercial traffic. Recently the home of the Pearse brothers has been restored by the Dublin Civic Trust. Pádraig Pearse (1879–1916) was an educationalist, a writer and a revolutionary, but is best known for his role in the Easter rising, for which he was executed. He wrote extensively in both English and Irish, and in 1908 he founded a bilingual school, St Enda's, with the aim of fostering all things Irish. Originally his nationalism was more cultural than political but he eventually came to the conclusion that force was needed in the face of Unionist opposition to Home Rule.

Pearse Street was once a very busy commercial street with theatres and department stores, but these are now gone, replaced by office developments and buildings erected by Trinity College as part of its expansion eastwards. The Garda Station, built originally for the Dublin Metropolitan Police, is a large building designed in the Scottish Baronial style. It is now the main police station for the south city. Sited on an awkward corner with Townsend Street to the rear, the building manages to turn the corner successfully with the use of a curved bay. An unusual feature of the building is the 'keystone cops', corbelled heads of policemen used to support segmental arches over the doorways. Maintained in good condition, this is an interesting building often overlooked by Dubliners.

PEARSE SQUARE
Also named after Pádraig Pearse, this is a small Victorian residential square near the Grand Canal Docks.

PEMBROKE STREET
Originally part of the Fitzwilliam estate, subsequently inherited by the Earls of Pembroke.

PERCY PLACE
Named after Hugh Percy, third Duke of Northumberland and Lord Lieutenant in 1829–30. Nearby Northumberland Road is also named after him.

PETER STREET
Named after the long-demolished St Peter's Church that once stood near here. Until recently, Peter Street was the location of the Adelaide Hospital which has now amalgamated with several other Dublin hospitals and moved to Tallaght. Nearby Peter Row is a laneway to the rear of the site of the demolished church.

PHOENIX STREET NORTH

Named for its proximity to the Phoenix Park. Before the completion of the quays, it was probably part of the main route to the park via Benburb Street.

PIG LANE

So named because of its links with the pork trade. In 1798 it was also called Pig Town.

PIGEON HOUSE ROAD

In 1761 John Pigeon was appointed caretaker of a blockhouse erected to store tools and materials along the South Wall, which was built by the Ballast Office. By 1765, the blockhouse was known as Pidgeon House. Pigeon and his family also provided refreshments for cross-channel passengers and those on excursions to view the construction of the South Wall. In 1793, the Pigeonhouse Hotel was erected to provide accommodation for passengers. This imposing cut-stone building still exists. Various uses have been made of the lands around this area, and the military had a fort here until 1897. After their departure, the Corporation bought the property. At this time, the Corporation supplied electricity to the city and it eventually constructed a power station here, which opened in 1902. This continued to operate until 1972, when the current Poolbeg Station superseded it. The old buildings remain, an industrial relic of a previous age.

PIM STREET

Possibly named after the Pim brothers, who were members of the Society of Friends and owners of a large department store on South Great George's Street.

PIMLICO

An area of narrow streets and small houses built as a scheme by the Artisans' Dwellings Company. The name came from a London street and was brought over by woollen merchants who settled here in the early 18th century.

PLEASANTS STREET

Opened in 1821 and named after the Carlow-born philanthropist Thomas Pleasants (1728–1818), who had opened an asylum for female orphans in Camden Street.

POOLBEG STREET

In the 15th century this was a long lane that led to a small pool (in Irish, poll beag) which was one of the deep anchorages of Dublin harbour. In the early 1700s, William Mercer was given permission by the City Corporation to infill behind Hawkins Quay, thus forming the Mercer Dock quayside, and later, after more infill, Burgh Quay and George's Quay. The line of Mercer Dock is now Poolbeg Street.

Mulligan's pub was founded in 1782 and retains much of its original character, with its low ceiling and wooden bar. Because of its proximity to the former *Irish Press* offices, it was a popular haunt of journalists and writers. The rear room was the setting for a scene in James Joyce's *Dubliners*.

PORTLAND PLACE / ROW / STREET

Named after the third Duke of Portland, Lord Lieutenant in 1782. At the junction where Portland Row meets Amiens Street stands the well-known Dublin landmark, the 'Five Lamps', erected as a memorial to General Henry Hall. Aldborough House, the home of the Earl of Amiens, was built in Portland Row in 1786.

PORTOBELLO HARBOUR

Like the Portobello area of London, Dublin's Portobello was named to commemorate the capture of Porto Bello in the Gulf of Mexico from the Spanish by Admiral Vernon in 1739. Formerly there was a harbour at this spot on the Grand Canal near Rathmines, but in 1948 it was largely filled in. A hotel opened on the harbour in 1808, run by the canal company – it was one of five along the canal between Dublin and the Shannon. Passenger services ended in 1852 but the hotel remained in business until 1860. It was later converted to the nursing home where the artist Jack B. Yeats spent his last years. It is now a college.

PRUSSIA STREET
Named after Frederick the Great of Prussia in 1765. It was previously known as Cabragh Lane.

QUEEN STREET

Located in the Smithfield area and probably named after Queen Elizabeth I, who reigned from 1558-1603. Queen Street leads to the former Queen Maeve Bridge. The King's Hospital or Blue Coat School was founded here before moving to Blackhall Place in 1669. The street is mostly given over to furniture showrooms.

RAGLAN ROAD

Takes its name from Fitzroy Somerset (1788–1855), Lord Raglan, a general in the Crimean War. Many of the roads in this area are named after military campaigns or figures. The poet Patrick Kavanagh (1904–67) lived in this area, which was dubbed 'Baggottonia' by his friends. 'On Raglan Road' is one of Kavanagh's most popular poems.

RAILWAY STREET

Once known as Great Martin's Lane, this was Mecklenburgh Street in 1733 and was renamed Tyrone Street in 1887, before finally acquiring its present name for its proximity to Amiens Street Station (now Connolly Station) and the railway yards. It is located in the former notorious 'Monto' area, synonymous in the 19th century with prostitution.

RAINSFORT STREET

Named after Sir Mark Rainsfort, an alderman of the city and Lord Mayor in 1700. Rainsfort had a lease on land here that was later leased to Sir Arthur Guinness for 9,000 years at an annual rent of forty-five pounds. The James's Gate brewery continues on these lands to this day.

RED COW LANE

A narrow street linking North King Street and Brunswick Street, probably named after a bar or tavern of this name.

REDMOND HILL

A corruption of the original Redman's Hill, this is a short street linking Aungier and Wexford Streets.

RIALTO

This name was originally given to Harcourt Bridge over the Grand Canal because of its supposed resemblance to the Rialto Bridge in Venice, but it was later taken to refer to this area on the South Circular Road.

ROBERT STREET

Named after John Robartes (Lord Robartes), Lord Lieutenant in the period 1669–70.

ROCK LANE

Off Baggot Street and probably named after the rocky gallows mound that was near here. This was also the origin of the name of Mount Street.

ROGER'S LANE

Off Baggot Street and named after Andrew Rogers, a grocer at 137 Baggot Street from 1818 to 1850.

RORY GALLAGHER CORNER

At the entrance to Meetinghouse Square, in Temple Bar. Rory Gallagher (1948–95) was born in Ballyshannon, Co. Donegal, but his family moved in the early 1950s to Cork, where he spent his formative years. Gallagher is rated as one of the most influential and passionate blues/rock performers of all time. Self-taught, he first achieved acclaim as the leader of Taste, an enormously successful late-1960s rock trio. He died in London in June 1995 from complications following a liver transplant.

RORY O'MORE BRIDGE

This was originally the site of the second bridge to be built across the Liffey. A wooden structure, it was built in 1670 and was known as Bloody Bridge. Several attempts were made to destroy it while it was under construction because of the financial damage it was likely to cause to ferry owners. Twenty men were arrested and taken to Dublin Castle. Most of them were rescued during a transfer to the Bridewell Prison, but four died in the process thus giving it the name of Bloody Bridge. In 1704 the stone Barrack Bridge replaced the previous structure, although it was still popularly known as Bloody Bridge. The current cast-iron bridge with stone piers was opened in 1861 and is one of the Liffey's finest bridges, clearing the river in one span. In the late 19th and early 20th century it was known as Victoria (sometimes Victoria and Albert) Bridge. It was renamed Rory O'More Bridge in 1922 after one of the ringleaders in a plot to capture Dublin in October 1641. O'More (1620–52) had initiated the conspiracy, but forewarned that the plot was discovered, he fled and managed to lead an insurgent army to victory in November 1641 at Julianstown, Co. Meath.

ROUNDHEAD ROW

While 'roundheads' was the name given to the Puritans during the reign of Charles I, this street did not get its present name from the Corporation until 1876. It was previously known as Cut-throat Lane.

ROYAL CANAL BANK

A terrace overlooking a former spur of the Royal Canal which led to the Broadstone Basin and supplied Blessington Street Basin. It is now a linear park.

RUSSELL STREET

Named after the builder John Russell, who died in 1825. The writer Brendan Behan (1923–64) lived at No. 14 as a child, in a house owned by his grandmother, who lived in nearby Fitzgibbon Street.

ST ANDREW'S STREET

This was known as Hog Hill until 1776, after the Abbey of the Blessed Virgin Mary del Hogges, but it was renamed after the Church of St Andrew which had existed here from medieval times. The present church was built in 1860-62 by W. H. Lynn and replaced an earlier oval Gothic church designed by Francis Johnston.

ST AUGUSTINE STREET

Designed by Pugin and Ashlin and named for its proximity to the Augustinian Church of Saints Augustine and John on Thomas Street.

ST JAMES'S WALK

Overlooking the former spur of the Grand Canal that led to the City Basin with its harbour, and to nearby St James's Infirmary. The canal's uses were threefold: to supply the City Basin with water, to enable Guinness to despatch barrels of stout and porter by barge to the midlands, and to supply the brewery with the water required for the brewing process.

ST JOHN'S ROAD WEST

Named after St John's Well in Kilmainham and built in the 1870s to allow access to Kingsbridge (now Heuston) Station. The well (now gone) was a place of pilgrimage and gatherings for many centuries, and the tradition of visiting the well on the feast of St

John the Baptist continued in one form or another into the early part of the 20th century.

ST MARY'S PLACE

Named after the church in the centre of the road known as the Black Church, whose black calp limestone turns jet when wet. In the title of his autobiography, *Twice Round the Black Church*, the poet Austin Clarke (1896–1974) referred to the popular myth according to which to run around the church three times at midnight would involve an encounter with the devil on the third round! The church, officially St Mary's Chapel of Ease, was designed by George Semple in 1830 and has a muscular Gothic exterior topped with tapering finials and a fine slender spire. The interior is one of the most original in Dublin, with its single parabolic arch making the walls lean inwards from floor level. It was said to be the favourite church of the English poet John Betjeman (1906–84), who was press attaché with the British Embassy in Dublin during the Second World War.

ST MICHAEL'S HILL

This was named after the church which once stood in the area and was demolished in 1787. The tower of St Michael's was incorporated into the Synod Hall designed by George Street and built in 1874. Street linked this building with Christ Church Cathedral (which he had restored) by means of a Gothic enclosed bridge spanning Winetavern Street, making the latter one of the most unusual streets in the city. The different origins of the two buildings is apparent in the two styles of stonework. Street designed the Synod Hall with a series of set-backs in such a way that although the main hall is of similar height to the cathedral, it looks lower than and subservient to, the main complex. The building is now the venue for a display on medieval Dublin. Although converted for modern use, many of the interiors remain intact, especially those of the hall itself and the adjacent meeting rooms. There is a fine view over the city from the top of the tower.

ST MICHAEL'S CLOSE

A narrow street on the slopes below the former St Michael's Church. It was once crossed by a stretch of the city walls with a gateway called the Porta Gillemeholmac. The street was then known as Macgiolla Mocholmóg Street, named after the chief ruler of Dublin 1125–34.

ST MICHAN'S STREET

Named after the two local churches dedicated to the martyr St Michan, the Roman Catholic church on Halston Street and the older Church of Ireland on Church Street. The street was known as Fisher's Lane in 1320; it has been called St Michan's Street since 1890.

ST NICHOLAS PLACE

Previously Arundel Court after Robert Arundel, who rented property here from the Corporation. It was later known as City Market and Blackhall Market. Its present name is attributable simply to its proximity to Nicholas Street.

ST PATRICK'S CLOSE

Beside St Patrick's Cathedral, this is the site of various buildings ancillary to the cathedral including the Choir School (in existence since the 1400s), the Dean's Residence and Marsh's Library. In the past the homes of many of the clergy were located here as well as in the now vanished Canon Street. Canon Street ran from the Close to nearby Bride Street, and was a narrow laneway of some twelve houses named after the minor canons of the cathedral.

Marsh's Library was designed by Sir William Robinson, Surveyor General from 1670 to 1700 and architect of the Royal Hospital Kilmainham. The library was set up by Archbishop Narcissus Marsh (1638–1713) as the first public library in Ireland. The interior, with its beautiful dark oak bookcases with carved and lettered gables topped by a mitre, remains unchanged since it was built nearly three hundred years ago. It is a magnificent example of a 17th century scholars' library, with its three original reading 'cages' or elegant wired alcoves into which readers were locked to prevent them from stealing the valuable books. Dean Jonathan Swift, author of *Gulliver's Travels*, spent much time studying here.

The library's extensive collection of books was built up from private bequests and collections. There are four main collections, consisting in total of 25,000 books relating to the 16th, 17th and early 18th centuries. As one might expect, there is a large collection of liturgical works, missals, breviaries, books of hours of the Sarum use, bibles printed in very many languages, and a great deal of literature on theology and religious controversy. The scope of the subjects is surprisingly wide and varied. There are books on medicine, law, science, travel, navigation, mathematics, music, surveying and classical literature in all the collections. A separate room is reserved for books and periodicals relating to Irish history and printed in the last hundred years.

The most important single collection is the library of nearly 10,000 books belonging to Edward Stillingfleet (1635-99), Bishop of Worcester, for which Narcissus March paid £2,500 in 1705. This was regarded as the finest private library in England in the later part of the 17th century. Other major collections include those of Dr Elias Bouhereau, a Huguenot who fled from France in 1695 and became Marsh's first librarian, and John Stearne (1660-1745), Bishop of Clogher, in addition to Archbishop Marsh's own personal library.

ST PAUL STREET
Named after the local church and parish of St Paul created in 1697 out of the parish of St Michan. The Church of Ireland Church closed in 1989.

ST STEPHEN'S GREEN

Named after St Stephen's Church and leper hospital, sited from 1224 to around 1639 in the vicinity of Mercer Street. 'The Green', as it is popularly known, was first shown on a map in 1655 and appeared without boundaries. In the early 17th century it consisted of about sixty acres, with access from a lane that later became Grafton Street. In 1664, the Corporation marked out twenty-seven acres and divided the remainder into lots for development, and by 1669 it was surrounded by a high stone wall.

By the 18th century the four malls outside the Green had acquired names. The north, south, east and west sides were known respectively as Beaux Walk, Leeson's Walk, Monk's Walk and French Walk. The principal entrance to the park was directly opposite York Street. In 1814 Commissioners were appointed to improve the square, enclose it with gates and railings, and allow access only to householders paying a guinea a year. In 1877 Sir Arthur Guinness (later Lord Ardilaun) succeeded through an Act of Parliament in having the area placed under the control of the Board of Works. It was re-opened to the public in 1880.

Lord Ardilaun (1840–1915) is among those commemorated by a statue in the Green, erected in 1892 in recognition of his bearing the cost of its lay-out as a public park. Along the west side is a statue to Robert Emmet, facing his birthplace. Others are of James Clarence Mangan, Thomas Kettle, Countess Markievicz, James Joyce and O'Donovan Rossa. At the Leeson Street/Earlsfort Terrace entrance is a monument entitled 'The Three Fates', donated by the German people in acknowledgment of post-war distress relief from Ireland. Fusiliers' Arch, at the main entrance facing Grafton Street, commemorates the Dublin Fusiliers who died in the Boer War, and whose names are inscribed on the underside of the archway. The Merrion Row corner has a sculpture depicting Wolfe Tone and a Famine memorial.

The architectural development around the perimeter of St Stephen's Green was somewhat piecemeal, since the owners of the lots were not obliged to build houses. This meant that by the early 18th century the Green was home to graveyards and breweries as well as dwellings. The northern side is notable for two fine buildings, the United Services Club and the Kildare Street and University Club, as well as for the Shelbourne Hotel. Both clubs have elegant interiors with ornate plasterwork. The Shelbourne Hotel is Dublin's most famous hotel, still very much a hub of social life in the city, with journalists, politicians and business people mixing in its bars.

The Eastern side of the Green is mostly office accommodation, some of which has been rebuilt in pastiche Georgian. Iveagh House, originally two houses, was donated to the state by the Guinness family in 1939 and is now the Department of Foreign Affairs. One of the original houses was designed by Richard Cassels in 1736. After Benjamin Guinness bought them in 1862, he acted as his own architect and produced the current single house. Finished in Portland stone, the building has a severe appearance. It has nine bays, the central three of which are broken forward and pedimented. The interior of the building is hugely elaborate and decorative with an extraordinary staircase and ballroom, both lined with alabaster. The staircase has ornate Victorian ironwork, marble columns and circular roof lights. Unfortunately the building is not open to the public.

Further along St Stephen's Green, Newman House is more obviously made up of two houses, joined in the mid-19th century but lacking a unifying façade, although both are faced in granite. The smaller house (No. 85) was known as Clanwilliam House and was designed in 1738 by Richard Cassels. When first completed it was free standing; it was also one of the first houses in granite on the square. The much larger No. 86 is five bays wide and four storeys high. At ground level both houses are rusticated with pedimented first floor windows, and both have outstanding interiors. The combined house was named after Cardinal Newman (1801–90), first head of the Catholic University, which later became University College Dublin. This was the original site of the university. It was here that Gerald Manley Hopkins was based in the Chair of Classics and where he died in 1889. Many of his papers were destroyed after his death as his colleagues were unaware that he was a poet and so no care was taken.

No. 86 St Stephen's Green was the residence at the end of the 18th century of Thomas Whaley, also known as Buck Whaley and 'Jerusalem' Whaley. The latter nickname came from his laying a bet that within the space of one year he could make the journey to Jerusalem on foot (except where a sea passage was unavoidable), play ball against the city walls and return, also on foot. As the ballad ran:

> 'One morning walking Arran Quay
> A monstrous crowd stopped up the way
> Who came to see a sight so rare
> A sight that made all Dublin stare.
>
> Buck Whaley, lacking much some cash
> And being used to cut a dash
> He wagered full ten thousand pound
> He'd visit soon the holy ground.'

Whaley won his bet!

Next door to No. 86 a small porch in rich polychromatic brick marks the entrance to University Church. Supported between the two houses is an unusual belfry. Cardinal Newman commissioned the church in 1856 from his friend John Hungerford Pollen in the Byzantine style, because of Newman's dislike of Gothic. The interior is richly decorated with an ornate altar, an arcaded gallery with screens and an elaborate pulpit. Small windows set under the roof light the church.

Beautifully sited on St Stephen's Green West, the Royal College of Surgeons in Ireland was built in two phases. The original building designed by Edward Parke consisted of the last three southern bays of the existing structure, and extended to a depth of five bays along York Street. This was absorbed into the later building of William Murray, a prominent bank architect and cousin of the architect Francis Johnston. Murray added four bays to the north and moved the pediment to the new centre of the building. The façade is distinguished by large round-headed windows separated by free-standing columns. The pediment shows the Royal Arms and is capped by three statues designed by John Smyth: Athena, the goddess of wisdom and war; Asklepios, the god of medicine; and Hygeia, the goddess of health. The interior of the building is very elaborate, with an impressive hallway and top-lit staircase with plasterwork in the style of Adams. Also of note is the boardroom by Parke. The RCSI played a central part in the Easter rising of 1916 when it was occupied by rebel forces led by Countess Constance Markievicz. The building remained relatively unscathed, but bullet holes are still visible on the stonework.

SACKVILLE PLACE
Originally named Tucker's Row after George Tucker, City Sheriff in 1731; and also known at one point as Mellifont Lane, from the famous monastery of Mellifont Abbey, which became the residence of the Earls of Drogheda. It was renamed Sackville Place in the 1750s after Lionel Cranfield Sackville, first Duke of Dorset, after whom O'Connell Street (Sackville Street) was named for a time.

SAMPSONS LANE
Off Henry Street and formerly known as Bunting Lane, this was named after Michael Sampson, City Sheriff in 1710–11.

SANDWITH STREET
Sandwith Street follows the line of the old high tide shoreline of

the Liffey before the building of the quays. In late 18th-century maps it is referred to as The Folly and The Folly Road. It was also known as Sandwich Street in a map of 1800, and was probably named after Joseph Sandwith, a merchant whose name appears in *Wilson's Dublin Directory of Merchants and Businessmen* of 1792–1810.

SARSFIELD QUAY

Named after Patrick Sarsfield (1655–93), Earl of Lucan and Jacobite military commander. A grandson of Rory O'More, after whom a nearby bridge is named, he was a very capable military leader, recapturing Connaught and helping to negotiate the Treaty of Limerick after the Jacobites were defeated at Aughrim. Afterwards he left Ireland and joined the French army, and was killed at the battle of Landen in Flanders. Constructed in 1766, the quay was previously known as Pembroke Quay and was renamed around 1886.

SCHOOL STREET

Prior to 1803, this was known as Crilly's Yard. Its present name probably reflects the establishment of a school here early in the 19th century.

SCHOOLHOUSE LANE

Named after St Anne's Schoolhouse built here in 1757. The western end is now called Molesworth Place.

SCHOOLHOUSE LANE WEST

Known in the 15th century as Le Ram Lane until the schoolhouse was built in the 16th century. At one time there were three Ram Lanes leading off High Street.

SEÁN HEUSTON BRIDGE

Now virtually unused since a new bridge was built beside it to cope with heavy traffic, Heuston Bridge (then King's Bridge) was opened in 1828. Nearby Heuston Station was known as Kingsbridge Station, but in 1966 both were renamed in honour of Seán Heuston, one of the sixteen executed leaders of the Easter 1916 rising. The bridge, of iron construction supported by two granite piers, was designed by George Papworth who also designed several banks in Dublin. It forms one great arch composed entirely of cast metal, one hundred feet in diameter. The piers are of handsomely cut mountain granite. It was called King's Bridge because £13,000 was collected for the purpose of raising a national monument to commemorate George IV's visit to Ireland in 1821.

The former Kingsbridge Station was commissioned in 1846 from Sancton Wood, an English architect. Easily the most impressive of Dublin's four railway termini, it is based on the design of an Italian palazzo, with a central block of nine bays masking the train shed designed by Sir John McNeill. This block has projecting Corinthian columns, balustrades and an attic storey, all decorated with carved swags and urns. To either side of this main block are domed campaniles. To the south is the main entrance block, built along the side of the railway shed.

SEÁN MACDERMOTT STREET
Named after one of the signatories of the 1916 Proclamation of the Republic. The street was previously known as Gloucester Street North, and before that as Great Martin's Lane.

SEAN O'CASEY AVENUE
Named after the playwright Seán O'Casey (1880–1964), who was born near here at 85 Dorset Street. It was previously called Rutland Street after the Duke of Rutland, Lord Lieutenant from 1784 to 1787. O'Casey spent much of his life in this part of the city, living in Innisfallen Parade, Dominick Street, and at various addresses in the East Wall area. At the age of forty-four, he gave up

his job as a labourer to concentrate on writing. On 10 February 1926, two days after the opening of *The Plough and the Stars* (which later became one of O'Casey's best-known plays), riots broke out at the Abbey Theatre in protest and chairs were thrown on to the stage. The police were called in to restore order and W. B. Yeats addressed the audience:

> 'You have disgraced yourselves again. Is this to be an ever-recurring celebration of the arrival of Irish genius? Synge first, and then O'Casey. The news of the happenings of the past few minutes will go from country to country. Dublin has once more rocked the cradle of genius. From such a scene in this theatre went forth the fame of Synge. Equally the fame of O'Casey is born here tonight. This is his apotheosis.'

O'Casey left Ireland to go to England where he married the Irish-born actress Eileen Carey. He died in Devon at the age of eighty-four.

SEVILLE PLACE / TERRACE
Seville Place, a long section of the North Circular Road, seems to derive its name from the capture of Seville by the British in the Peninsular War in 1812.

SHERRARD STREET
Named after the Sherrard family, official surveyors to the Wide Streets Commissioners. Members of the family acted as surveyors and clerks and prepared maps in their official capacities as well as operating a private practice.

SHIP STREET, GREAT
This is a corruption of the medieval name of Sheep Street, referring to a grazing ground. It was also once known as Polemill Street, after the pool and mill at the monastery founded here in the 6th century. Leading down to one of the rear gates of Dublin

Castle, it became a street of tenements, with the Poddle river flowing alongside. The river was covered over in the 19th century. The buildings on Ship Street were built in the 19th century as accommodation for Army engineers. Over the years they were put to a variety of uses, serving as offices and for training purposes. By the 1980s they had become derelict, abandoned and vandalised. The Office of Public Works has now renovated the buildings, creating a streetscape inside the castle compound and restoring the façades. Virtually unknown, the buildings are notable for their variety of doorways and windows. They now face across a paved open area to the new Chester Beatty Library of Oriental Art.

SHIP STREET, LITTLE
Originally know as Pole or Poole Street because of the nearby pool which supplied a monastery on this site with water. The river Poddle fed the pool through the area which is now Great Ship Street.

SIGARD ROAD
Like this one, many streets of housing built by the Artisans' Dwellings Company in the Oxmantown area were named to a pattern based on Irish and Norse history and mythology.

SITRIC ROAD
Named after Sitric Silkbeard, the son of Olaf Cuaran, who became king of Norse Dublin around 989 and held the position until 1036 despite being defeated at the battle of Clontarf in 1014. The first to mint coins in Dublin, he was also responsible for founding Christ Church Cathedral around 1030. Olaf Road is nearby.

SIR JOHN ROGERSON'S QUAY
This is named after the property developer Sir John Rogerson, who was Lord Mayor in 1693–4 and who built the quay wall, reclaiming the former mud flats and slob lands behind it. Having

received fee farm rights to the slob lands in 1713, he commenced work on the wall in 1716 to protect them from flooding. This land was bounded by the Liffey, the Dodder, present-day Bath Avenue, Grand Canal Street and Creighton Street, and was a substantial holding. Rogerson died in 1724.

SMITHFIELD

In 1664 the city assembly ordered that 'part of Oxmantown-green be taken and set by lots in fee farm – reserving a highway and large market-place'. This resulted in the large market space of Smithfield and the smaller nearby Haymarket, both named after areas of London. Smithfield has in recent years become the focus of a scheme of urban renewal, and the massive space designated as the Dublin Civic Plaza has been resurfaced and now features tall gas-fired braziers.

SOUTH CIRCULAR ROAD

Started in 1763, and stretching for four-and-a-half miles to part-ring the city like the North Circular Road, the South Circular consists mainly of Victorian brick houses. It took years to complete these two roads, and the work was extended as a relief scheme to provide employment. The ring roads run almost parallel to the two canals, explaining why canal bridges seem to occur near so many junctions on the main routes out of the city. The South Circular Road was until recently the location of Griffith Barracks, formerly Wellington Barracks. This is now a college, but the militaristic wind-vane on the cupola of the main stone block can still be seen.

SOUTH CUMBERLAND STREET

Although once a country lane, there have been buildings on Cumberland Street and nearby Boyne Street since the 17th century. It is named after the Duke of Cumberland.

SOUTH GREAT GEORGE'S STREET

Originally known as St George's Lane, this street is named after the church dedicated to St George that stood here in 1181 and was rebuilt in 1213 after it became incorporated into the Priory of All Hallows. A busy commercial street with many Victorian buildings, South Great George's Street once contained many department stores, now all closed.

The street's main landmark, the South City Markets, takes up an entire block and is surrounded on all sides by a network of small commercial streets. The building is heavily ornate in terracotta and red brick, and originally contained a large glass-covered marketplace. After a serious fire in 1892, this was destroyed and replaced to a cruciform plan, with intersecting arcades. The interior has since been remodelled. One of the arcades became incorporated into a small factory unit and a department store (now vanished), but the remaining arcade gives a good impression of the original intention.

The adaptation after the fire was handled by W. H. Byrne, who was also responsible for removing the central tower and spire and the corner spires from the George's Street façade. At the same time, he designed several blocks of shops in the streets behind the complex, with shopfronts modelled on the façades of the Markets building. The original entry arches can still be seen on the building. The arcade is top-lit by glazed panels in the rood and by clerestory windows. The complex also has a huge columned and vaulted basement, now a public car park. The building came under threat in the 1970s but was reprieved and has gained a new lease of life since the market became a busy pedestrian route.

SOUTH LOTTS

The name given to the area bounded by City Quay, Tara Street, Gloucester Street South and Sandwith Street. The plots were divided out in 1723, and each lot went to the highest bidder. Since then the name South Lotts has come to refer to a wider area, extending as far as the Grand Canal Docks.

SPENCER STREET / SPENCER DOCK

Named after Earl Spencer, Lord Lieutenant from 1868 to 1874 and again from 1882 to 1885. He formally opened the dock himself.

STAMER STREET

Named after the former Sheriff and Lord Mayor of Dublin (1819–20) Sir William Stamer, who died in 1838.

STANHOPE STREET

Dating from 1792, it is believed to be named after one of two Stanhopes who consecutively held the office of Viceroy in Ireland. Philip Dormer Stanhope, Earl of Chesterfield, was Viceroy from 1745 to 1747; his kinsman William Stanhope, first Earl of Harrington, was his immediate successor.

STANLEY STREET

Named after the family of Sir Thomas Stanley, who owned the manor of Grangegorman. Now a short cobbled cul-de-sac, the street was originally intended to be longer.

STEEVENS' LANE

The former Dr Steevens' Hospital stands here, now the headquarters of the Eastern Health Board. Both the hospital and the street were named after Dr Richard Steevens (1653–1710) who bequethed his estate to his sister with the instruction that upon her death it should be used to build a hospital for the poor and destitute. His sister however decided to fund the hospital out of the estate herself, taking only a small annual stipend. Dr Steevens' Hospital was the result, founded in 1717.

Based around a courtyard plan, the internal space recalls the nearby Royal Hospital (Kilmainham), which predates it, only on a smaller scale. The interior courtyard has arcaded walks around the perimeter. (It featured in the Definitive Stamp Series issued in the 1980s by An Post, based on Irish architecture through the ages.) An unusual feature are the brabazons across the corners, which were a later addition. Edward Lovett Pearce may have been responsible for the design of the boardroom, although this is not absolutely certain. Further up Steevens' Lane is St Patrick's Hospital founded by Jonathan Swift.

STEPHEN STREET
Named after the old church of St Stephen, which also gave its name to St Stephen's Green. It is a meandering street whose origins as a country laneway show. For many years it was the location of the Dunlop pneumatic tyre factory, and the fine curved Art Deco Dunlop building still exists as offices.

STIRRUP LANE
Probably named after a family who resided in this area.

STONEYBATTER
Derived from the Irish *Bothar na gCloch* or 'Road of the Stones', Stoneybatter was once one of the main routes out of the city, a village in its own right bordering Oxmantown Green.

STORE STREET
After the construction of the Custom House in 1792, a new dock was also built on its eastern side, as were some stores for holding merchants' wares. These stores existed until the 1940s when they were demolished. In the early part of the 20th century the Old Dock (as it was known) was filled in, although it had been suggested at one point that it might be used as an underground car park. Eventually the filled-in dock site was partly used for the

construction of Busáras and for Memorial Road, which extended the crescent of Beresford Place around the Custom House to meet the river again at the site of the more recent Talbot Memorial Bridge.

Designed by Michael Scott (1905–89) and his team of young architects and designers between 1945 and 1953, Busáras was one of the first post-war examples of the International Modern style in Europe. It was built against a background of public opposition centered on its external appearance, function and excessive cost – over £1m before completion in 1953. The design was inspired by the work of Le Corbusier, notably the Maison Suisse (1930–31) in Paris and his use of elements like pilotis, glazed façades and a pavilion on the top storey. One of the most important characteristics of Scott's work was his integration of art and architecture, a key feature of Busáras. He always tried to incorporate art and sculpture into his buildings because he felt that the different disciplines complemented each other. Scott's interest in textures and colour represented a move away from the stark white modernism of the 1930s. This is also reflected in the interior design of the Busáras building, with the use of many different materials and surface finishes.

SUFFOLK STREET
This was the site of the Viking assembly mound known as the Thingmote. It survived here until it was removed in 1685 (the earth was used in raising the level of Nassau Street to prevent flooding). Named after Sir Thomas Howard, Earl of Suffolk, it was also the site of the family home of the Earls of Kildare before James Fitzgerald built Leinster House.

SULLIVAN STREET
Named after T. D. Sullivan, Lord Mayor of Dublin in 1886 and 1887.

SUMMERHILL / PARADE / PLACE

Part of the Gardiner estate, Summerhill has been widened in recent years to create a dual carriageway, losing all signs of its antiquity in the process.

SWEENEY'S TERRACE

Located off Mill Street and named after the Sweeney family who were merchants there. Until 1932, Sweeney's Terrace had some good examples of houses in the Dutch Billy style. It was originally entered from Mill Street through a narrow gateway.

SWIFT'S ALLEY

Named after a 17th-century merchant, Goodwin Swift.

SYCAMORE STREET

Known as Sycamore Alley until 1869, this was where a Dublin institution began in 1846 when Joshua Bewley opened his first coffee-house. It later transferred to nearby South Great George's Street. In 1916, Bewley opened another branch in Westmoreland Street, followed by one in Grafton Street in 1926.

SYNGE LANE / PLACE / STREET

Probably named after the family of Edward Synge, Bishop of Elphin, who owned property here. George Bernard Shaw (1856–1950) was born at No. 3 Upper Synge Street, now 33 Synge Street. The house is now the Shaw Museum and is open to the public. Shaw left Dublin in 1876, determined to become a novelist, and returned to Ireland only for short visits thereafter. He was awarded the Nobel Prize for Literature in 1924, and was made a Freeman of Dublin in 1946. He left a third of his estate and royalties to the National Gallery of Ireland where he is commemorated with the Shaw Room. He wrote: 'I am one whose whole life was influenced by the Dublin National Gallery for I spent many days of my boyhood wandering through it and so learned to care for art.'

SYNNOTT PLACE

Dating from 1795, this was called after a family of that name who owned property here. Mark Synnott of Drumcondra Lane (now Dorset and Bolton Streets) was Sheriff of the County of Dublin in 1742.

TALBOT STREET / PLACE

Named after Charles Chetwynd, third Earl of Talbot and Lord Lieutenant 1817–21. This is a busy commercial street, a continuation of Earl Street North, off O'Connell Street. Previous names were Cope Street North and Moland Street. Moland was the name of a family registered together with the Deverell family as co-owners of property in the area. This is the origin of the name of Deverell Place, off Lower Gardiner Street at the rear entrance to the Department of Education. Moland Place, dating from 1840, preserves the Moland name.

TARA STREET

This was developed in 1885 as a completely new street on the site of previous streets known as Shoe Lane (part of which was also called Stocking Lane) and George's Street. There was also a flea market here. The new street was named after Tara, the capital of the ancient Kings of Ireland. In Rocque's map of 1756 it is marked as George's Street, presumably because it led to George's Quay. Tara Street was widened in 1932 when Butt Bridge became a fixed construction, having previously been a swing bridge which could open to accommodate boat traffic on the river. The fine Central Fire Station of 1900 designed by C. J. McCarthy with its fine Italianate brick campanile has recently been amalgamated into a hotel development.

TEMPLE BAR

Before the quays were constructed, this street corresponded to the riverbank of the Liffey estuary. It was written 'Temple Barr', and was the site of the gardens and mansion of Sir William Temple, Provost of Trinity in 1609. The street has since given its name to the entire area bounded on the north and south by the river Liffey and Dame Street, and to the east and west by the old Houses of Parliament (now the Bank of Ireland) on College Green and Parliament Street. During the 1960s and 1970s Córas Iompair Éireann (CIÉ) acquired much of this site and planned to build a major new urban bus dépôt. The plan was abandoned, and the government eventually established Temple Bar Properties to develop the area to a cultural and architectural brief. A limited competition held to establish the architectural framework in 1991 was won by Group 91 Architects, a loose grouping of young architectural practices. As a result of the area's cultural brief, many galleries, archives and exhibition spaces have been built, including the Irish Film Centre, the National Film Archives, the National Photographic Archives, a multimedia centre and a cultural centre for children known as the Ark.

TEMPLE BAR SQUARE

This is one of three new public spaces created in recent years in Temple Bar, the others being Curved Street and Meetinghouse Square. Temple Bar Square was created by setting a new range of buildings back from the existing line of the street. The open square in front of the buildings is rather windswept, with a few trees and light fittings. As a public space it has been less successful than Meetinghouse Square, which is used for public events and markets.

TEMPLE LANE

Named after Sir William Temple, whose mansion and lands were once sited here. In Brooking's map of 1728 it was known as Dirty

Lane. It is now part of the cultural precinct of Temple Bar.

TEMPLE STREET

In 1886 the lower end of the street was renamed Hill Street because of the area's poor image.

TENTERFIELDS

A tenter is a machine for stretching cloth by means of hooks. The area was the centre of Dublin's weaving industry, giving rise to this and other local place-names such as Weavers' Square.

THOMAS STREET / COURT / LANE

Modern Thomas Street corresponds to what in ancient times was the *Slighe Mór*, one of the great roads crossing Ireland which met at the ford of the Liffey known as Áth Cliath. The street was later named after the nearby Augustinian friary of St Thomas à Beckett, founded in 1177 by order of King Henry II. It was originally St Thomas Street, but the prefix was dropped. The abbey is believed to have been in the vicinity of St Catherine's Church, stretching back to South Earl Street. The name of the abbey is also perpetuated in Thomas Court, Thomas Lane and Thomas Court Bawn. After the suppression of the monasteries in 1537, the lands of the friary passed to the Brabazon family, who later became the Earls of Meath.

There has long been a strong brewing and distilling tradition in the Liberties area and nowhere is this more apparent than in Thomas Street, where John Power began distilling in 1791. The fine buildings he developed survive today. They include offices along the street and large granary buildings, which are now used by the National College of Art and Design. Inside, remnants of the site's industrial past are still visible, with steam beam engines and other remains scattered throughout the college. Unfortunately only three of the large vats survived the demolition of the building in which they were housed.

Further along Thomas Street is the spot where Arthur Guinness started his large and famous brewery, while across the road was the distillery (now part of Guinness) owned by the Roe family. This is the site of Ireland's largest windmill, now minus its sails. Henry Roe is best remembered for having funded the cost of the restoration of Christ Church Cathedral in the late 19th century.

There are many fine buildings in Thomas Street including an old fire station, various commercial premises and two churches, the 18th-century St Catherine's and the 19th-century Church of Saints Augustine and John. Designed by John Smyth in an austere Doric style, St Catherine's never acquired the spire originally intended for it. The building was derelict for many years but has recently been cleaned and restored. It has a fine galleried interior. It was outside St Catherine's that the patriot Robert Emmet was executed in 1803.

The Church of Saints Augustine and John boasts the tallest spire in Dublin, visible all over the city. It has what is probably the most dramatic façade of any church in Dublin. In part funded by the Power family, the building was designed by George Ashlin and Edward Welby Pugin, son of the famous Victorian architect Augustus Welby Pugin. Construction started in 1862, but the interior was not completed until around 1911. The church is a massive polychromic Gothic Revival structure of red sandstone, limestone and granite, its entrance framed by a massive arch surmounted by the spire with its collection of colossal sculptures. There is a fine interior with lavish decoration on the main altar and in the side chapels. An intended transept was never built.

THOMAS DAVIS STREET
Named after the Young Irelander Thomas Davis (born 1814), who died from an attack of scarlet fever at the age of thirty-one. From a

Protestant and military background, Davis was educated at Trinity College before becoming a founder of *The Nation* newspaper in 1841. Although a poor public speaker, he was the undisputed leader of the Young Irelanders because of his personal charisma and the strength of the articles he wrote. He was a keen advocate of the revival of the Irish language as a means of reversing the anglicisation of Irish culture.

THOR PLACE
Like so many of the streets of artisan housing developed in this area, Thor Place was named to a pattern based on the names of figures from Norse and Irish history and mythology.

TOLKA QUAY
Named after the river Tolka which flows into Dublin bay here. The Tolka is about thirty kilometres in length and rises near Batterstown in Co. Meath.

TOLKA QUAY ROAD
Originally a quayfront created after the reclamation of land in the docklands. It was named after the river Tolka, whose course where it flowed into the bay was altered by this development. Since then even more land has been reclaimed and the street has lost its river frontage.

TOWNSEND STREET
Originally this was a ridge that lay above the tidal area of the Liffey and was used as a landing place by the Vikings, who marked it with a pillar known as the Long Stone erected at the junction of the now underground river Steyne and Liffey. Because the land sloped down to the river on the north side (and to a lesser extent on the south side also, to the marshy land that is now Trinity College), the area became known as Lazers' Hill or Lepers' Hill. The reference to Lazarus or lepers was because this was an

assembly point for pilgrims – often lepers – embarking for Santiago de Compostela in north-western Spain. Townsend Street's present name probably comes from a Lord Lieutenant and General Governor of Ireland, Viscount George Townsend, although it may also derive simply from 'town's end', as published in a map by Andrew Yarranton in 1674.

TRINITY STREET

So named because at one time there was a hall of residence for students of Trinity College here. Until 1756 it was known as Trinity Lane.

USHER'S ISLAND

This name comes from John Ussher (1524–90) who leased this former island from the Corporation in 1557. Ussher was Sheriff in 1557 and Mayor in 1561, and in 1572 he sponsored the first ever book printed in the Irish language. The Ussher home was in the vicinity of Bridgefoot near Bridge Street (not to be confused with Bridgefoot Street, further west), and its gardens and grounds occupied much of the surrounding area. In 1664, the land of Usher's Island was granted in a further lease to Sir William Ussher (1601–71) of Bridgefoot, and it was his son Christopher who took the initiative of building Usher's Quay and Usher's Island Quay and filling in Usher's Pill (a small bay or pool on the Liffey shoreline). Christopher Ussher's son William further developed the two quays and was known as 'of Usher's Quay' showing that the use of the name was now commonplace. Many of the Ussher family were to play a role in the development of Dublin, and held various offices including those of sheriff, mayor and alderman. Arthur Wellesley, Duke of Wellington, was a great-great-grandson of Sir William Usher.

Bounded by two branches of the river Camac, and what was known as Ussher's Pill and on the north side by the river Liffey, the land was effectively a small island. After construction it was known for a time as Usher's Island Quay but that has now been shortened. James Joyce's story 'The Dead', from *Dubliners*, was set in No. 15. The film version also was shot in this house, which is currently undergoing restoration after years of neglect.

USHER'S QUAY

This is also named after the Ussher family, whose home was sited nearby. Moira House, one of Dublin's finest houses, stood here until the early 20th century. It was the residence of the Rawdon family, to whom the baronetcy of Moira was given in recompense for services rendered to the Stuart cause. The fourth baronet became Earl of Moira in 1762 and embellished the interior of Moira House in a style of great splendour. John Wesley wrote that he visited Lady Moira in 1775 and 'was surprised to observe though not a more grand, yet a far more elegant room than any he had seen in England.' This was an octagonal room with a window, the sides of which were inlaid with mother-of-pearl. When Lord Edward Fitzgerald was hiding from arrest, Lady Pamela Fitzgerald was received by the Dowager Countess of Moira, and was here on the evening her husband was taken. Moira House was maintained as a family mansion for some years after the death of the Countess in 1808, before passing into the hands of the Governor of the Institute for the Suppression of Mendicity in 1826. It was occupied by Seán Heuston during the 1916 rising.

USHER STREET

Referred to in Rocque's map of 1756 as Usher's Lane. Named after the Ussher family, it probably conforms to what was the southern edge of the former Usher's Island.

VALENTIA PARADE

Reflects a naming pattern in this area, with streets named after places in Co. Kerry.

VERNON STREET

Like nearby Portobello Harbour, Vernon Street commemorated the victory of Commodore (later Admiral) Edward Vernon over the Spanish at Porto Bello in the Gulf of Mexico. Vernon served as Commander-in-Chief of all the king's ships in the West Indies and was known as 'Old Grog' because of the grogram (coarse fabric of silk, mohair and wool) overcoat he wore. Vernon recognised that there were too many sailors under his command going blind and dying of alcohol poisoning. He therefore cut their rum ration by half. This watered-down rum saved many a seaman's life and came to be known as 'grog', thereby introducing a new word into the English language. Vernon bragged that he could take Porto Bello with five ships, and did so in 1739 in an expedition from Port Royal. London's Portobello Road got its name as a result. Mount Vernon, an estate on the banks of the Potomac River in the United States of America, was also named after Vernon. This was owned by Lawrence Washington, who fought under Vernon's command. When Washington died in 1752, Mount Vernon passed to his half-brother George, later America's first President.

VERSCHOYLE PLACE

Probably named after Barbara Verschole, to whom Richard, Lord

Viscount Fitzwilliam was friend and patron. Verschoyle Place lies between Upper and Lower Mount Street. Barbara Verschole died in 1837 at the age of eighty-five. According to a plaque in Booterstown Roman Catholic Church of the Assumption, she was instrumental in persuading Fitzwilliam to provide the church for the use of his tenants.

VICAR STREET

A narrow street off Thomas Street, it acquired its name for its proximity to the former friary of St Thomas à Beckett.

VICTORIA QUAY

During Queen Victoria's visit to Ireland in 1863, she opened the new bridge at Watling Street and this quay was named in honour of her visit. Victoria Quay is now entirely occupied by the giant Guinness brewery which began to develop here in 1873, moving northwards from James Street.

VICTORIA STREET

This was Kingsland Park until 1876 when it was renamed after Queen Victoria.

VIKING ROAD

Named to reflect the Norse heritage of this part of the city known as Oxmantown or Ostmantown, to which the Vikings were banished after the Anglo-Normans gained control of Dublin.

WAPPING STREET
Probably taken from the area of London with the same name.

WARDS HILL
Named after the Ward family who had a brewery here and on New Row.

WARREN STREET
Named by the Artisans' Dwellings Company after Robert Warren, one of its directors.

WARRENMOUNT
Named after Nathaniel Warren, Lord Mayor in 1782, who owned a brewery in nearby Mill Street. He built a residence here called Warrenmount on the site of the mills that gave Mill Street its name, which were granted to William Brabazon in 1536 after the dissolution of the monasteries.

WASHINGTON STREET NORTH
Named after George Washington (1732–99), first President of the United States. The street was previously Washington Row.

WASHINGTON STREET SOUTH
Named by three developers – Peter Doyle, Miles Breslin and Michael Fleury – who returned from the USA and purchased land here, in the early 19th century.

WATERLOO ROAD

Named after the battle of Waterloo, in which the Duke of Wellington defeated the Emperor Napoleon of France. The names of many of the streets in this area have a military ring. They include Wellington Road, which runs parallel.

WEAVERS SQUARE / STREET

The centre of the weaving industry in Dublin, which was mainly in the hands of Huguenot settlers.

WELLESLEY PLACE

Named after Richard Colley Wellesley, Lord Lieutenant from 1821 to 1828 and again in 1833–4.

WELLINGTON QUAY

This was the last of the city quays to be constructed. It was built around 1812 and replaced a row of houses built right to the river's edge. It was named after Arthur Wellesley, later Duke of Wellington (1769–1852), who was born in Merrion Street. Wellington spent most of his career in the military (in the revolutionary and Napoleonic wars between England and France) and in politics outside Ireland, although he sat in the Irish Parliament as MP for Trim from 1790 to 1795. He was a Tory Prime Minster from 1828 to 1830. Not proud of his Irish background, he once famously said that 'being born in a stable does not make one a horse'.

WELLINGTON ROAD

One of the main roads in the Phoenix Park and named for its proximity to the imposing Wellington Monument, built to commemorate the victories of Arthur Wellesley, Duke of Wellington (known as the Iron Duke), who was born in Dublin. Completed in 1861, this is the tallest obelisk in Europe at 205 feet. It was originally intended to be even taller but had to be restricted because of lack of funds. The memorial includes four bronze plaques cast from cannons captured at Waterloo, three of which feature pictorial representations of Wellington's career, while the fourth bears an inscription. The plaques are: 'Civil and Religious Liberty' by John Hogan; 'Waterloo', by Thomas Farrell; and 'The Indian Wars' by Joseph Kirk. There were also plans for a statue of Wellesley on horseback, but the shortage of money ruled this out. There is another Wellington Road in Ballsbridge, close to Waterloo Road.

WELLINGTON STREET

Like nearby Nelson Street, also named after a military hero, this is named after the 'Iron' Duke of Wellington. It was previously called Paradise Row.

WERBURGH STREET

Named after the medieval church of St Werburgh which took its name from Werburgh, Abbess of Ely, who died around 700 AD. The original church was built around 1178, but was damaged by a fire in 1754 which left only the tower and façade intact. The present building dates from around 1759. The body of the church was the work of Thomas Burgh, but it is believed that the main west façade – more detailed than would generally be typical of Burgh – was designed by Alessandro Galilei during his visit in Ireland to design Castletown House in Co. Kildare. The fine tower and spire of St Werburgh's was removed in 1836 by the authorities in Dublin Castle, which the church overlooked, because they feared it might be used by subversives or snipers in time of rebellion. They claimed however that they were taking this step on grounds of safety – although they ignored the architect Richard Johnston's offer to make the tower safe.

The church has a fine galleried interior with oak panelling. Located in a relatively unfashionable area, it escaped the attentions of Victorian 'restorers' and many of the original features remain, including the clear glazing. The gothic pulpit was originally designed by Richard Johnston for the Chapel Royal in Dublin Castle.

Off Werburgh Street was Hoey's Court, where Jonathan Swift, author of *Gulliver's Travels,* was born at No. 7, the home of his uncle. It is now a cul-de-sac leading to an unemployment exchange for men.

One of the last cagework, timber and plaster houses in Dublin existed on the corner of Werburgh and Castle Streets, before it was demolished in 1813.

WESTLAND ROW

Originally known as Westlands after William Westland who owned property in the area. One side of this street at the rear of Trinity College is now completely occupied by various departments and faculties of the college. In recent years Trinity has also developed modern buildings behind the existing Victorian houses. The street has some noteworthy buildings, including Kennedy's pub located on the corner with Lincoln Place. Formerly Conway's, this is mentioned in the works of Samuel Beckett and James Joyce, and with its ornate terracotta, it boasts one of the finest pub exteriors in Dublin. Near it, facing down the length of the street, is Sweny's Pharmacy, where in Joyce's *Ulysses* the character Leopold Bloom buys a bar of lemon soap.

The western side of Westland Row is mostly made up of Victorian houses with terracotta decoration at parapet level. The eastern side is dominated by the Church of St Andrew, built with the assistance of Daniel O'Connell between 1832-7 and designed by James Bolger. At No. 36 is the Royal Irish Academy of Music, which was founded in 1848 and moved here in 1871. The house was built around 1771 and was the residence of the Duke of Conyngham. It features plasterwork ceilings by Michael Stapleton. Westland Row Station (now Pearse Station) was the terminus for the Dublin-Kingstown railway, reputed to be the first commuter railway in the world when it opened on 17 December 1834.

WESTMORELAND STREET

Leading from College Green to O'Connell Bridge and named after John Fane, tenth Earl of Westmoreland and Lord Lieutenant from 1790 to 1794. One of the last streets to be laid out by the Wide Streets Commissioners, Westmoreland Street was designed as part of a set-piece with D'Olier Street, the two meeting at the bridge. Plans were originally sought in 1792, and those submitted by Henry Aaron Baker (Gandon's one-time assistant) were accepted in 1799. The original development was of four-storey brick buildings over shops at ground level. Some of these still exist but most have been replaced by Victorian developments.

WEXFORD STREET

A gateway to the Liberty of St Sepulchre once stood here.

WHITEFRIAR STREET

So named because of the Carmelite Monastery, which has been here since the 1200s. The original monastery was built by Sir Robert Bagot in 1278 but was dissolved in 1539. Unlike other suppressed orders, the Carmelites eventually returned to their original location, building a new monastery here between 1765 and 1816. Designed by George Papworth, the church is entered from Aungier Street beneath the monastery accommodation. It has a fine interior but is best known for containing the remains of St Valentine, given by Pope Gregory XVI to Fr Spratt in 1835.

WHITWORTH ROAD

This road is a memorial to Charles, Earl Whitworth, who was Lord Lieutenant in 1813-17 but was more famous as Ambassador to France after the Peace of Amiens. The former Whitworth

Hospital and Whitworth Bridge, now Fr Mathew Bridge, were also called after him. Whitworth Road was known popularly as the Bishop's Road, as it adjoined the property of Charles Lindsay, last Protestant Bishop of Kildare, who died in 1846. Nearby Lindsay Road and Crawford Avenue (he was son of the Earl of Crawford) also commemorate this family.

WICKLOW STREET

Originally part of Exchequer Street, but the inhabitants of this part of the street petitioned the Wide Streets Commissioners to have the name changed because of its bad reputation, which made it difficult for them to find respectable tenants for their properties. The name was changed on 18 October 1837. It is now a busy shopping street.

WILLIAM STREET NORTH

Both North William Street and Clarence Street are called after William, Duke of Clarence, afterwards William IV.

WILLIAM STREET SOUTH

Named after the developer of the street, William Williams, who laid it out in 1676. The street is dominated by Powerscourt House, which was designed by Richard Cassels and built in 1774 at a cost of £80,000 for Richard Wingfield, the third Viscount Powerscourt. The gateway on the right of the house led to the stables; the one on the left to the kitchen and other offices. Hardy, in his *Life of Lord Charlemont*, says that Powerscourt was one of the few men of high rank who resided almost constantly in Ireland, and not more from attachment than from duty. On his death in 1788 he was laid out in state in the house, and the public were admitted for two days to view the body. Richard, fourth Viscount, sold the house to the Crown for £15,000; it was used by the Commission of Stamp Duties in Ireland until 1811. Once a fashionable residential street, William Street is now the centre of the clothing trade. Powerscourt Town House was converted to a shopping centre in 1981.

WILTON TERRACE / PLACE

Named after Wilton in Salisbury, the seat of the Earl of Pembroke and Montgomery. Wilton Place was originally two terraces around a triangular park facing the Grand Canal, but only six of the original brick and granite houses remain. The original railed park remains in the centre, with an unusual 19th century cast-iron fountain. Wilton Terrace faces the Grand Canal but none of its original houses remains as they were all demolished to make way for two office blocks. The poet Patrick Kavanagh, who lived around this area for much of his life, is commemorated by a seat on the Mespil Road canal bank beside the lock. There is also a life-sized statue of him sitting on a bench on the opposite bank.

WINDMILL LANE

So named for a windmill which once stood in the area, illustrated in several engravings dating from the early decades of the 19th century.

WINETAVERN STREET

One of Dublin's oldest streets, dating from the 11th century or earlier. It was mainly occupied by taverns and was referred to in old documents as 'Vicus Tabernariorum Vini'. With the exception of some buildings at the lower end of the street it has been completely redeveloped in recent years, and the eastern side is occupied by Dublin Corporation's offices on Wood Quay. During excavations of the area a pattern of Viking streets and houses was discovered. Paving setts laid out in the pavement near Christ Church Cathedral at the upper end of the street display the arrangement of walkways and walls excavated.

WOLFE TONE STREET

Wolfe Tone Street was formerly Stafford Street after Sir Hugh Stafford who developed the area with Sir Humphrey Jervis, but it is now named after the patriot Theobald Wolfe Tone (1763-1798), who lived at No.44 as a child. From a prosperous Protestant background, Tone was educated at Trinity College and qualified as a barrister. He believed that Irish Protestants, Catholics and Dissenters (Presbyterians) should unite in pursuit of what he saw as their common interests. In 1791 he produced a pamphlet entitled, 'An Argument on behalf of the Catholics of Ireland'. Because of his activities with the United Irishmen, he was eventually forced to leave Ireland for the United States, from where he travelled to France. There he persuaded the French to send an expedition to Ireland in support of an insurrection. He sailed in September 1798 but was captured off the Irish coast. After his trial, he committed suicide in prison while awaiting the death sentence.

The park alongside Wolfe Tone Street was once the churchyard of St Mary's Church, designed by Sir William Robinson. An architectural competition was held in 1998 to redevelop the space as a public plaza.

WOLFE TONE QUAY

Also named after Wolfe Tone, this quay runs along the site known as Croppies' Acre, the burial spot of some of the rebels executed after the 1798 rebellion. A small memorial park has been built on part of the site. Up until the 1840s, when the river was realigned and this quay and Victoria Quay were constructed, the Liffey ran closer to Benburb Street, past the burial ground in front of the former Royal Barracks, now Collins Barracks. With the construction of the quays around the 1860s it was named as Albert Quay (to correspond with Victoria Quay opposite). The Quay was renamed around 1940.

WOOD STREET

Named after the Reverend Daniel Wood, curate of St Stephens Church in 1634.

WOOD QUAY

Wood Quay is the oldest quay in Dublin, with wooden piles and earthen banks being used to push the tide back here from around 900. By around 1300, a stone wall had been constructed, roughly along the south side of Wood Quay. The reclaimed area was used for housing, and over the years further dwellings were built over the previous ones. In 1587 the worst disaster in Dublin's history occurred when gunpowder recently unloaded at Wood Quay was ignited. Over 200 people were killed in the explosion.

In 1968 an architectural competition was held for the design of new headquarters for Dublin Corporation on Wood Quay, on a site earmarked for the purpose since the 1950s. The winning design was the work of the architect Sam Stephenson. (Michael Scott came second with a scaled-down version of the UN building in New York, complete with plaza, podium and fourteen-storey glass-sided block.) Stephenson's design consisted of four monumental granite-clad blocks linked by a glass atrium. The two blocks at the rear of the site were to be taller, allowing the building to descend towards the river. After construction began, however, remains from the Viking city were found preserved beneath the site, as well as a long section of the medieval city walls. This turned out to be the most important discovery linked to Dublin's Viking origins that had ever been made, and one of the most important Viking sites anywhere in Europe.

After a period of some years of court cases, site invasions, excavations of the site and much publicity, the Corporation finally began to build. Their nerve did not hold in the face of public protest, however, and after Phase 1 was finished, the remainder of Stephenson's project was put on hold, never to be fully executed.

The ground around the two blocks was landscaped and the remains of the city wall piled up in a basement. In the late 1980s another competition was organised to complete the development and erect a building along the quay. It was won by the firm of Scott Tallon Walker, and the project was finally completed in 1994.

YARNHALL STREET

A yarn hall was built here as part of an extension to the nearby Linen Hall in 1716. The remains of a gateway still exist.

YORK STREET

Situated midway along the western side of St Stephen's Green, York Street was named after Ernest Augustus, Duke of York and Albany who died in 1728. It was once quite a fashionable street, but the original houses have now all disappeared. One side is occupied by the Royal College of Surgeons; the other is taken up with Corporation housing and a Salvation Army hostel.

ZOO ROAD

Named after Dublin Zoo, founded in 1830 and after London the second oldest zoo in Europe. In the 1980s and early 1990s there was a campaign to try to have it closed because of its general dilapidation and the cramped conditions of the animals, many of whom were exhibiting signs of stress. Recent investment has resulted in a huge expansion of their space and facilities. The zoo boasts of having bred the famous MGM lion.